Getting Started

★

David Allen

Inland Valley Daily Bulletin columnist

Pelekinesis

Getting Started by David Allen

ISBN-10: 1-938349-49-0
ISBN-13: 978-1-938349-49-2
Library of Congress Control Number: 2016952698

Book Design by Mark Givens
Front Cover photo by John Valenzuela
Photos pages 245-256 Tom Zasadzinski/Inland Valley Daily Bulletin

First Pelekinesis Printing 2017

For information:
Pelekinesis
112 Harvard Ave #65
Claremont, CA 91711 USA

www.pelekinesis.com

Getting Started

David Allen

Contents

Foreword 13

Introduction
Finding my way 17

Ah, the joys of packing up and moving
May 25, 1997 25

Interleague play sparks romance
July 6, 1997 29

Ladies and gentlemen, just barely live, the Molding Stones!
November 16, 1997 33

Redecorating the interior of a plane
January 18, 1998 37

Hard work is a moving experience
March 1, 1998 41

Does the job market have you at the end of your rope?
March 22, 1998 45

Today's topic: Baby goes to the dentist
April 26, 1998 49

'Da bomb' takes on a whole new meaning in Chino
May 24, 1998 53

Raise the curtain for the not-so-great films of the century
June 21, 1998 57

Now who'll believe his big scoops?
June 24, 1998 61

Scaling new heights, not looking down
July 22, 1998 65

'Sorry, wrong number' calls are pushing his buttons
July 26, 1998 69

Flash! Gays rampant; U.S. in a panic!
August 5, 1998 73

Waiting for a tow, time sure passes slow
August 26, 1998 77

The bald facts on sheriff's hair apparent
September 2, 1998 81

Don't play it again, Sam — please, don't
October 14, 1998 85

There's a 'Closed' sign on the California Welcome Center? That's a fine how-do-you-do
December 2, 1998 89

Don't have a cow, man! Chino jury duty limited to sitting, waiting, preserving democracy
December 16, 1998 93

Latest megamerger joins Christmas, Thanksgiving; deal may contain sanity clause
December 23, 1998 97

ITEMS! 101

A 1990s guessing game: Is this clothing store for men, women or both? (or neither?)
January 27, 1999 109

Angry bees are 25 years late, but the 10-year-old boy in all of us still says: Killer!
February 24, 1999 113

$166 million too much for a park? Hah! Why, Rancho Cucamonga is aiming too darn low
March 10, 1999 117

Feelin' less groovy at 35, as pop culture — Lauryn who? — slips away
March 14, 1999 121

Who was that masked man? It could be a wrestler, as lucha libre invades Pomona!
March 31, 1999 125

Lose your keys? Simple problems turn us into morons
April 25, 1999 129

Jury duty in sliding-door injury case was trial of the century, in a manner of speaking
May 12, 1999 133

If you've got the Time, they've got the subscription offer
May 16, 1999 137

How do we develop the Chino Valley dairyland? First, we tell the cows to moooooove
May 26, 1999 141

Class clown? Him? Awful truth revealed
May 30, 1999 145

Men! Boys! Pick up women without even breaking a sweat
June 27, 1999 149

Ontario's street planters seem like a roundabout way to slow down speeding traffic
June 30, 1999 153

If cops and firefighters get own Olympics, give other professions a sporting chance
July 7, 1999 157

Readers offer straight talk on roundabouts, say Police Games no laughing matter
July 21, 1999 161

Shortened workweek in France makes him bleu
July 25, 1999 165

Salmonella-plagued dining hall needs fixing, and Dave's got some eggs-citing plans
September 29, 1999 169

Comic Mort Sahl is no longer hip, but as Claremont gig shows, he's still got that edge
November 17, 1999 173

Students wait for their '60 Minutes' of fame at media-besieged Walnut High
November 24, 1999 177

Earth to Mars: Give back our missing probes!
December 12, 1999 181

Rats! 'Peanuts' is ending, and that's one thing you can't be wishy-washy about
December 15, 1999 185

More ITEMS! 189

Funny thing about the new game show craze: rich in prizes, but poor in smarts
January 12, 2000 195

In South Carolina, enthusiasm for the defeated Confederate banner doesn't flag
January 26, 2000 199

Real Rancho Cucamonga not exactly 'Simpatico' with two recent movie portrayals
February 9, 2000 203

Blah blah blah yak yak yak
February 13, 2000 207

Here's an umbrella theory on why guys do dumb, manly things — like get rained on
February 16, 2000 213

Movies, media go cuckoo for Cucamonga
February 20, 2000 217

Time passing too fast? Try spending it waiting in line
March 12, 2000 221

'Titanic' star's success in journalism gives columnist sinking feeling
April 12, 2000 225

Sorry, Peter: 'Jaws' still has its bite
April 16, 2000 229

Going for broke, Upland spares no expense on its way to the poorhouse
April 19, 2000 233

Central Coast is high on Rancho Cucamonga's Los Osos school name
April 26, 2000 237

Who said Central Park couldn't be done? Oh yeah, the voters did
May 17, 2000 241

He boldly goes where no columnist has gone before — work, 2020 style
May 21, 2000 245

Please, just photo shoot him now before the future arrives
May 21, 2000 253

Wrestler Rowdy Roddy Piper turns out to be a hard man to pin down
May 24, 2000 257

To those who believed in me, thanks for your support.
To those who didn't, thanks for making me try harder.

Foreword

David Allen is a curious fellow with a curious job. He was the shy nerd with an appreciation for the ridiculous, longing to be the class clown. Then he picked up pen, er struck typewriter key, er touched computer key and set his fingers on a mission to show the world the unbeatable combination of a wily brain and a way with words.

I was his editor for a time on the *Inland Valley Daily Bulletin*, and oh what a time. Reporters tend to come in two flavors, ones who ask good questions, others who write well. This guy could do both. Since I'm not an idiot, I became an advocate for his column writing, which reached readers in such indelible ways.

Dave makes you laugh because he is interested in you, the life around you and the town you live in. He's not just phoning it in, he has the patience to look for the real story. He has an eye for detail through voracious reading, keen observation, off-the-charts empathy and regularly walking his neighborhood. And yours.

He embraces the everyday weirdness; delights in the quirkiness that makes the towns he covers like nowhere else.

Dave actually knows where the funny bone is. He's the guy who knows that Swaziland, Africa was hiring for a hangman, the Seminole Indians in Florida were in need of an alligator wrestler and European filmmaker Roman Polanski once ran a classified ad looking for a leading man.

His is a sharp wit, wielded gently. (Although the laughs are likely to be out loud … at least mine are.)

He once dared ask the question "Precisely how hot is it in Hades?" when Inland temperatures were soaring, proving just how far he would go for readers: "I visited hell. Climbing into a handbasket — the fastest way to get there, I'm told — I was transported through Time and Space until landing with a thud in what appeared to be an underground cave."

In another brave search to get answers for his readers: "Since prime-time game shows are now a bonafide phenomenon, over the weekend, risking irreversible brain damage, I watched all four."

He uses such nifty words and phrases as: "pell-mell style," "retain affection for his weedy boyhood home," "creepy musical motif," "I thought each night, head upon my pillow, smiling dreamily as the veil of slumber descended."

You'll see in this set of columns that Dave was an early adopter of the inevitable: "Capping a frenzied year of corporate mergers, Santa Claus announced today that Christmas is merging with Thanksgiving, a move that will create a $2.2 trillion megaholiday. Under pressure to produce profits, Claus stunned the financial world with his acquisition of Thanksgiving, rumored at $600 billion. Wall Street reacted favorably to the news, sending shares of Christmas soaring. 'This is a real win-win.'"

An early adopter of interactive journalism: "The latest scientific research tells us that, when confronted by the unexpected, we begin acting, in medical jargon, like bozos. Say we can't find our keys. (Readers, in unison: 'We can't find our keys.')"

And he's always helpful: "Oops, didn't see you at first. I was rummaging around my desk, looking for our missing Mars lander."

Or: "Exactly why I was asked to help (a friend move) remains a mystery. I'm a journalist, which means my main form of physical activity is arching an eyebrow."

—Christia L. Gibbons,
associate faculty, Walter Cronkite School of Journalism and Mass Communication

September 2016

Introduction

Finding my way

By this point, it may seem as though I've always been at the *Inland Valley Daily Bulletin*, with 2017 marking my 20th anniversary at that august journal. But I haven't always worked there, or lived here. Hired as a reporter, I figured this would be like my three previous newspaper jobs, a gig to keep for three or four years before moving on to a slightly bigger and better paying paper.

But a funny thing happened on the way to fulfilling that plan — namely, I had become a full-time columnist, my original career goal, and there seemed no reason to give it up. No reasons have occurred to me since then either, and so here I am.

This book, my second, collects columns from my first four years at the *Bulletin*, 1997 to 2000. My first, *Pomona A to Z*, brought together columns from 2004-05 about Pomona. Chronologically, *Getting Started* is a sort of prequel, only without Darth Vader as a boy.

For background, I'm an Illinois kid who moved to the Bay Area after college for a job in comic books that taught me I didn't want to work in comic books; instead, I went into newspapers, having loved writing for my college paper at the University of Illinois, the *Daily Illini*, where I had a weekly humor column, Campus Scout. It was, if you'll accept my word for it, very popular, taking an irreverent tone toward college life and institutions.

In the working world, nobody starts off as a columnist, arguably the best job at any paper, and so I learned how to be a reporter while at a string of small papers in Sonoma County: the *Santa Rosa News Herald*, where I interned, followed by full-time jobs at the nearby *Rohnert Park-Cotati Clarion* and *Petaluma Argus-Courier.*

I did contribute an occasional column at the *Clarion*, and the results were okay, but it was difficult transitioning from writing for a college audience, where everyone was about the same age and going through the same thing, to writing for an audience that might span 50 or more years, with me at the young end. I didn't have the life experience and, when I look back, I was so naive and ignorant about nearly every aspect of life it's a wonder I could button my own shirts.

Being a reporter, though, proved to be a lot of fun, even if my early assignments, like the mobile home rent control board, were not necessarily riveting. Local government became a specialty of mine as I covered first the city of Cotati, then Rohnert Park, then Petaluma, and as crafting stories, writing punchy sentences and injecting humor became my stocks in trade. My stretch at the *Argus-Courier* was probably the zenith of the news writing phase of my life as I competed for stories against the larger *Santa Rosa Press Democrat.*

Feeling stuck, though, after this series of low-wage jobs and knowing I needed to leave to move up a rung, I cast my resumes around the state and in 1994 was hired on at the *Victor Valley Daily Press*. Its location, Victorville, was pretty much the precise opposite of the gentle hills and balmy temperatures of Sonoma County. The politics were opposite too, conservative and pro-growth where Sonoma's were liberal and anti-growth. It was a good lesson in perspective. The pay was considerably better, as newspapers go, and the cost of living lower, making for a modestly improved quality of life. (Living it up, I bought my first TV.) The landscape, scenically and culturally, was arid, but the move did put me in Southern California.

I covered government for the *Daily Press*, first San Bernardino County and later some of the cities. After nearly two years there, an idea for a humorous essay came to me — the first such idea I'd had in years. I wrote it and it turned out all right. A second idea occurred to me. I asked if I could write a column every week, knowing I'd be more likely to keep writing if forced to by deadlines, and the editor said sure.

After three years, the chance to move on to Ontario and the *Daily Bulletin*, which had double the circulation, presented itself, and I was among a wave of hires in early 1997. I liked the idea of continuing a column, now that I had a vague sense of how to write one as a grown-up, and the editors were receptive, although a regular spot was not available.

And so, amidst council meetings and other assignments, I would file an occasional guest column for our Lifestyle section. They ran one or two Sundays per month as space was available. By spring 1998, a regular Sunday slot was given to me, and that summer, a Wednesday appearance was added.

It might seem I was on my way, and I was, I guess, although establishing myself was hard. In that first year at the *Bulletin*, in which I went from covering booming Fontana to babysitting quiet Upland to being exiled to the Lifestyle section, I lost all confidence, concluded I might have peaked professionally and considered quitting the business or returning to a smaller paper. Thank goodness I hung in there. Things got much better.

The circumstances under which these columns were written were challenging. My Wednesday column was in the News section and my Sunday column in Lifestyle, not that there was any particular aesthetic reason for the split. Meanwhile, I was still writing stories for Lifestyle, and to avoid conflicting with that full-time assignment, I was told my News column had to be written on my own time. Uh, okay. So much for the prestige of being a columnist.

There wasn't opportunity, really, to go out and interview people, or attend council meetings, or research local history, all things that later became hallmarks of my columns. Instead, I wrote a straight humor column. Many were cranked out at my newsroom desk in a couple of hours on a Saturday morning, riffing off weird items in the news.

This split-personality life ended in 2001 when I became a full-time columnist, and the more universal approach to humor gradually faded as my columns became more about local journalism than whimsy. These would be the sort of columns to which *Bulletin* readers — are you one? — have become accustomed.

For this book, I considered simply picking up from, say, 2005, where *Pomona A to Z* left off in a sense, and ignoring the earlier columns. Then again, why ignore what Woody

Allen, in *Stardust Memories*, called "the early, funny ones"? My hope is to produce a series of collections that will preserve columns and other writings that seem worth the book treatment. And if that's going to be the case, then I might as well go back to the beginning.

This required me to reread these columns for the first time in many years. In the meantime, I'd written nearly 2,000 columns. Taking a fresh look at the earliest ones was enlightening, and occasionally horrifying.

My influences were disparate and not entirely digested: Dave Barry and Robert Benchley, *Los Angeles Times* humorists Steve Harvey and Roy Rivenburg, the Bullpen Bulletins sections in old Marvel Comics and "Shouts and Murmurs" essays in the *New Yorker*.

Going back to these early columns was like reading the work of someone else, albeit someone whose outlook and sense of humor were familiar. Some columns were terrible, as I was clearly flailing around for a consistent tone or a worthwhile topic. Some were neither here nor there, bungled in some way or too dated.

Others were a pleasant surprise. When it came time to choose columns for this book, I went with my gut. If a column made me barf, I didn't pick it. But if I laughed out loud at least once, it probably made the cut. Also, nearly any locally themed column, or item from a column of brief pieces, had an edge simply because it might, in a small way, document the era.

Roughly one in four columns was deemed worthy. They're presented in chronological order but can be read in any order you choose. No item columns, as I call the ones made up of several short pieces, appear in full, but some individual items appear in two groupings later in this book. A few of the columns seemed to need context or brought back specific memories, and those are shared in mini-introductions sprinkled in the relevant places.

A few other columns from this period have been set aside for possible topic-oriented book collections about music, travel and more. But this book does include a music-themed column from 1997 postulating a Rolling Stones tour in 2017 — a notion ridiculous two decades ago — simply because the timing was perfect.

It's doubtful that many of you reading this book recall any of these columns, even if you did happen to read them 16 or more years ago, which was another plus for putting them into a book. This material will be new for nearly all of you.

Even though these columns are quite different than my more recent and familiar output, I hope you'll enjoy their silliness and look kindly upon various late '90s references and instances of ineptness therein.

If you laugh out loud now and then, that would be cool.

Ah, the Joys of Packing Up and Moving

May 25, 1997

Not that packing our household belongings turns us into morons, but during my recent move from Victorville, I stopped a helper from tossing out approximately 1/2 of one serving of Banana Nut Crunch, a cereal I don't even like.

"Hey, I'm going to need that!" I exclaimed, my voice rising.

My friend was dubious but indulged me, which is what friends are for. The first morning in my new apartment, I sheepishly ate that tiny bowl of cereal, most of which had been crushed into powder, just to prove my point, whatever it was.

How had it come to this? I had planned to comb through my belongings and weed out the junk, or at least the stale food, before packing.

Instead, I ended up frantically cramming everything into boxes at the last minute, without rhyme or reason.

Among the vital items I brought: pants I would have to lose 5 inches off my waist to wear again, a box of brown sugar solid enough to use as a doorstop, eye drops that expired in May 1994, etc., etc.

Why the last-minute rush? Perhaps I should start at the beginning.

Millions of years ago, the Earth cooled and dinosaurs roamed ... oops, too far back.

Actually, the fun began just a few weeks ago, when I accepted a job offer from the *Inland Valley Smog-Ledger*, or whatever we call this newspaper.

I figured I'd move to Rancho Cuckooclock — do I have that right? — because of its strategic location near my job, major freeways and the Souplantation restaurant.

With that settled, I spent a day checking out various apartment complexes, as advertised in the *For Rent* guide that can be found in finer gas stations everywhere.

Based on the photos and descriptions, most modern apartments are maintained well, painted pink and green, and named by cretins.

These apartments all have foo-foo, woodsy names like Wyndchyme Village or Mountain Lakeshore Forest Meadows or Wildflower Rainbow Unicorn Apartments — even though they never allow pets (how, er, pastoral) and sit half a block from a 7-Eleven.

Why can't we have honest apartment names, like Scary Neighbor Estates or Thin Wall Villas?

The *For Rent* photos are extremely flattering and may have been shot by the same shutterbugs who make Angela Lansbury look like a fresh-faced teenager. In many photos a scenic mountain is so close it practically sits next to the kiddie pool.

(Discreetly out of camera range are the carports, where

hairy-shouldered men in undershirts spend entire weekends changing the oil of their disabled 1970s gray-primer vehicles.)

In some of the photos, the complexes actually glow. Personal visits showed the glow actually radiates from the extremely cheerful leasing representatives.

They welcomed me, explained the ritzy qualities of their particular crackerbox palace and encouraged me to leave a fully refundable deposit right then to ensure that I could become a part of their "community."

Generally speaking, you don't find this level of heightened chirpiness outside a sorority.

But my resistance slowly eroded. By the end of the afternoon I had picked a place I liked, which led to my driving to a sleazy liquor store to buy a money order for my good-faith $100 deposit.

"That will be $104," the man behind the counter said with a thick accent.

"A hundred and forty dollars?" I asked in shock.

"Haha. No, $104. That would be a big profit, huh? Haha," the man said.

"Haha," I agreed, suppressing the desire to punch him in the nose. After a week in Florida — really; I had a vacation planned before I even accepted the job offer — I returned to Victorville, 31 hours before the arrival of the movers and with approximately 172 hours of packing to go.

With a friend's help, I began boxing my motley collection of mismatched dishes, Bob Dylan records and unread-but-classy novels, taping the boxes shut and not labeling them, which I lived to regret. And, naturally, not taking time to throw anything out.

Weeks later in my new digs, surrounded by piles of stuff, I'm still trying to get organized.

Although, come to think of it, I've been working on that for 33 years.

The next column was inspired by a crush on a co-worker of the era whom I found far too intimidating — beautiful and strong-willed — to approach. But, hey, combined with some sports news, my hopeless longing did inspire a bleakly funny column, and sometimes that's the best you can do.

Interleague Play Sparks Romance

July 6, 1997

So I took a break from clipping my toenails to think about interleague baseball and how this concept could be applied to your romantic life.

In case you hadn't heard, there's an exciting new development in baseball, a sport in dire need of excitement. Baseball games are so slow — how slow are they? — that by the "seventh-inning stretch" one or two veteran players have usually died.

To fans, this slow pace is part of the beauty. Baseball fans pay close attention to details, like tiny fluctuations in batting averages, but, typically, they fail to see the big picture. (Many also fail to bathe.)

Think of this: You can fail miserably two out of three times at bat, yet be the league's top hitter (at .333) and earn more than entire elementary school faculties. Although, to be fair, few teachers know how to turn a single into a double.

Standards are a little higher in basketball, where excitement is the watchword. In basketball, the action only stops so Dennis Rodman can get another body part pierced.

Major League Baseball, reluctant to admit it made a mistake and start from scratch with a new sport, such as competition rock-scissors-paper, keeps coming up with new twists in failed attempts to perk things up.

Among the innovations: the designated hitter, the night game, wild-card playoff berths, the San Diego Mesquite Chicken, Morgana the Overly Breasted Bandit, etc., etc.

The latest wrinkle is interleague play.

The way it used to work is, you had your two leagues, your National League and your Synonym-For-"National" League. Each league had its own teams and they played only against each other, so that succeeding generations of teams began looking more and more alike.

Now there is interleague play. A few times each season, one team from the National League and one team from the Synonym-For-"National" League will, in clear violation of the laws of nature, play against each other.

The results, we have been assured, "count." What a relief! I was afraid a baseball game wouldn't "count" for anything and would be merely a way to pass time!

This leads me to romance.

How many times have you felt a hankering for someone, only to conclude he or she was "out of your league"? (Gosh, I wonder where Mr. Allen's headed with this!)

Unless you're one of these model-like people, you know what I'm talking about. I'm talking about someone with nice straight teeth, a refined laugh, tastefully color-coordinated clothes, like that. You see them, you want to date them, but you know it will never happen because (sigh) they don't even know you're alive.

Don't blame them, though; it's not their fault.

It's sort of like a science fiction plot. See, the model-like people's atoms vibrate slightly faster than everyone else's, putting them on a different plane of existence where we can see them but they, strangely enough, cannot see us. Except in rare moments, such as when no other model-like people are around and they need a favor.

Sure, you would like to date them, but they — literally — do not know you exist. But under the David Allen Interleague Romance Concept, it will be possible to date these people.

Of course, this can only occur under tightly controlled circumstances. Why? Because I said so (slap slap slap).

Also, if Interleague Romance happened all the time, if all boundaries disappeared, there would in effect be no "leagues" at all and society as we know it would collapse, not that this would be a great loss, except for *Seinfeld*.

How it would work is, once each summer you would get one date — one! — with someone on the Out of Your League roster.

You (the dater) would file your request with the Commissioner of Romance, who would be Jenny McCarthy. Jenny would scheduled the date. The party Out of Your League (the datee) would have 15 days to accept or to present a valid medical excuse for canceling, such as that they were in a full-body cast after leaping off a 15-story building to avoid dating someone like you (i.e., you).

The actual date would occur on a baseball diamond inside a stadium filled with fans, who turned out because it's "Painful Mismatch Night" and they got a free cap. They would cheer for the person representing their league, either you or your date.

Unfortunately, and I haven't come up with a way around this yet, the person Out of Your League would always win the date.

Why?

Because you couldn't even get to first base.

Ladies and Gentlemen, Just Barely Live, the Molding Stones!

November 16, 1997

As long ago as 1977, rock fans wondered if each tour by the Rolling Stones would be the last. But proving the doubters wrong, that long-anticipated "farewell tour" only came today, in the year 2017.

About time, you say? You may be right. After all, Mick Jagger is now 74 and limits his public appearances to "prime rib night" at Coco's.

But the Stones are rolling around the globe one more time, aiming to give their fans some satisfaction (har!) and sop up any cash remaining after their '12 tour, dubbed "Steel Wheelchairs."

Last night they kicked off "The Last Time" tour in Los Angeles. The venue was the venerable Los Angeles Coliseum, which is vacant for the season since Al Davis Jr. moved the Raiders north again.

Fans spilled in for the opening act, the newly reunited Spice Girls, then waited with a mix of excitement and dread for the main attraction.

Would the Stones manage, against all odds, to keep their title as the world's greatest rock and roll band?

Certainly it looked to be a grand stage show, surpassing even the Stones' trend-setting efforts of the past. Ticket-holders could affix an electrode from their bleacher seat to their frontal lobe for a 4-D experience. The Stones also kept everyone on edge by paying for a two-hour shift of the Earth's magnetic polarity.

Plus, they had smoke machines.

Despite the grandeur, ticket prices were held down to $212 each, thanks to a lucrative tour sponsorship by Depends.

Suddenly, the stage lights dimmed, lasers fired and Mick and Co. took the stage to the thump of "Not Fade Away," an early hit obviously brought out by the aging rockers as a show of defiance to Father Time.

The thrill lasted for a nanosecond. You didn't need to look at the huge video screens to see the change in the band members' once-vital appearance.

Charlie Watts, 76, kept the beat behind the drum kit but was hooked to a respirator. Guitarist Ron Wood, the youngest Stone at 70, bobbed back and forth in a rocking chair as he squeezed out some licks.

The once-rambunctious Mick Jagger stood stock-still at the microphone, shouting the lyrics in a monotone and hanging on for dear life to his toupee.

Hopping around in the background, a manic grin on his creased face, only lead guitarist Keith Richards, 74, seemed healthy and fresh.

"Are you having a good time?" Jagger shouted at the audience, which murmured a vague reply.

In the hoariest cliche in the book, Jagger playfully cupped his hand behind his ear.

"I can't hear you!" he shouted.

It quickly became obvious that he wasn't kidding. He really couldn't hear them.

A stream of hits followed: "(I Can't Get No) Satisfaction," "Brown Sugar," "Start Me Up," and the most recent, "Grindin' Down (Don't Tell the Dentist)."

During the intermission, fans buzzed. The last tour wasn't shaping up quite the way anyone had hoped.

"Keith's looking good, though," a man next to me observed.

After the break, nurses led the Stones back to their instruments. Starting off the set with "Honky Tonk Women," Jagger managed to leap in the air and do a split when he hit the stage. Then he stopped singing and didn't move.

"Keith! I've fallen and I can't get up!" he screeched.

Next, the energy level dropped like a flatlined EKG with "The Spider and the Fly," another 1960s classic.

Naturally, the line about the groupie who was common, flirty and looked about 30 had to go.

"She was shady, a lady, she looked about 80," Jagger sang with a wink.

Digging into the band's musical roots, Keith performed a recent 12-bar number, the loping "Colostomy Bag Blues." The Stones closed the show with "Memory Mile," whose lyrics Jagger couldn't remember.

As we filed out of the Coliseum, a surprising number of us waited at the souvenir stand for one last memento: a Stones tour T-shirt with the latest variation on the "tongue" logo. Out of one corner came a stream of drool.

ᔓ ◈ ᔓ

The next column accompanied a feature story of mine about a deaf pilot, Henry Kisor, who had followed in the sky trails of Cal Rodgers, a hearing-impaired pilot who had flown cross-country in 1911. In 1995 Kisor started in New York and got as far west as Upland's Cable Airport but due to weather conditions couldn't continue to Long Beach. He wrote a book, *Flight of the Gin Fizz*, about the experience of becoming a pilot to shake off the middle-age blues.

In 1998, the *Chicago Sun-Times* journalist returned to Cable to pick up where he left off. For our interview, we sat in a quiet cafe on a rainy afternoon and he lip-read my part of the conversation. I realized I didn't need to speak above a whisper, just mouth the words, and he caught everything I said. When he took the flight, I was invited along. He wrote me after reading the column that he had no idea what had happened in the back seat. You'll just have to read to see what he meant.

Redecorating the Interior of a Plane

January 18, 1998

So when a colleague suggested that I go on an airplane ride with a pilot who's deaf, my reaction was probably the same as the deaf pilot's: "Could you repeat that?"

Nevertheless, a few days later I found myself at 2,500 feet with a pilot who had lost his hearing. Big deal: He found himself with a passenger who, before too long, had lost his lunch.

Actually, breakfast.

But I'm getting ahead of myself.

A ride with a deaf pilot, I thought, might make a good humor column — although not a great humor column. A great humor column would be riding with a blind pilot. Also a great obituary notice.

About the only humor potential I could see with a deaf pilot was that, if we did a mid-air roll or dive, I could communicate my discomfort by holding up a sign reading "Aaaiiieeeee!!"

Nevertheless, I agreed. And so I soon found myself aloft

with Henry Kisor in a Cessna fourseater, bound for Long Beach.

Up front were Henry and co-pilot Shawn Cate; in the back, me and perfect stranger Mary Barnett. (Well, perhaps not perfect — I don't want to put Mary on a pedestal.)

It was my first time up in a small plane since my boyhood, during the late Cretaceous Period, and for a few moments it was grand fun.

All the houses, streets, buildings, roads, cars and bushy trees looked fake, like those tabletop architectural models you find under glass in an office lobby with a plaque that says "Future Expansion."

Pretty soon we were flying over Disneyland, which from the air looks alarmingly small. (It's a small theme park after all?)

Then, trouble: Henry banked for a MAJOR turn west, causing my stomach to slide to a new part of my body, which fought to reject this organ transplant like it was a baboon heart.

Landing in Long Beach was a big moment of triumph for Henry, as those of you who read my Life story on page A17 well know. If not, take my word for it. Big moment of triumph. Real big.

All too quickly, though, we climbed back into the plane for the return flight.

Perhaps if I don't look out the window I won't get sick, I thought. So I pretended to be deep in contemplation on whatever was outside the window, while secretly keeping my eyes shut.

Closer to Upland, the skies were dark, even with my eyes

open. Radio traffic indicated we might be circling several minutes over Cable Airport because of planes from the air show.

This was not good news. I couldn't very well ask Henry to pull over by the side of the road.

Still, there was a peculiar satisfaction at the thought of flying over the City of Gracious Living and hurling.

We soon got permission to land, but Henry cut the engine too quickly and we kind of came down doing the Limbo. On the tarmac, Henry put on the brakes, or however it is you slow down a plane, and I felt my stomach shift again.

Next thing I knew, I was wearing my breakfast.

Shawn handed me an air sickness bag, but, to quote the old saying, that's sort of like giving someone a tetanus shot after he's already been bitten by Christian Slater. Mary slipped away to alert the appropriate authorities, probably by loudspeaker, and a man who is on Upchuck Alert came out to mop up.

"I've cleaned up lots worse than this," he said. Great, another failure.

In 10 years as a reporter this had never happened to me on a story. In fact, as a member of the media, I'm more used to my work making other people throw up.

Luckily, Henry didn't hear any of the commotion. I considered alerting him by holding up a sign that said "Raaaaalf!!", but that wasn't necessary. He knew all about my embarrassment.

After all, he still has his sense of smell.

Hard work is a moving experience

March 1, 1998

Hear that high-pitched whine? It's every muscle in my body screaming in pain.

Yesterday, as I write these words, I helped a friend move.

Today, I can't move.

If you want to get rid of any lingering illusions that you are physically fit, I heartily recommend spending a day moving someone's worldly belongings.

There's nothing like schlepping around boxes, sofas and dressers for a few hours to remind you just how pitifully out of shape you are.

Even a day later, my arms are sore and bruised. My shoulders sting. My hands are red and raw.

Pardon me while I (grunt) shift position on my deathbed.

Exactly why I was asked to help remains a mystery. I'm a journalist, which means my main form of physical activity is arching an eyebrow.

Journalists are famed as cigarette-puffing, gin-swilling,

stress-plagued slobs, although that image is becoming passe. Why, several of my colleagues have stopped drinking, mainly because lifting a glass leaves them out of breath.

So if you want help moving, don't call a journalist. Only call a journalist if you're not going to finish those fries.

In this case, though, the person who needed help moving is also a pad-and-pen type. My buddy Matt was moving from Orange County to Encino — insert your own joke here; I'm in too much pain — for a newspaper job. Matt is one of those friends who is always "there" for you, so it seemed bad, when he needed a hand, to be "somewhere else" for him.

The extent of his desperation became clear when I arrived that morning at his apartment in Placentia. The crew consisted of myself, Matt, his dad and two brothers. You could have put all of us together and gotten one regulation-sized set of muscles.

Refrigerator-moving duties were handled by the two biggest guys, while I busied myself by carrying more manageable items, such as light bulbs. Unfortunately, my return trips from the truck occurred at inopportune moments, which is how I ended up toting one end of a mattress.

There's no way to carry a mattress that doesn't make you look like a doofus. You look like even more of a doofus when you drop a mattress, as I learned, twice.

In fact, my fingers kept slipping out from under whatever object I was carrying. Every object I lifted seemed as smooth as a Clinton denial.

This wasn't all the fault of the objects. It was mostly because my idea of muscle definition is looking up the word "muscle" in the dictionary.

However, it's equally true that my friend and his wife, Jill, own some darn heavy stuff.

For instance, Jill packed her collection of shoes by dumping all of them into one oversized trash bag the size of a stove. Naturally, she could not move this bag herself. No man wanted to move it either, based on the manly beliefs that no one should own this many shoes, except Payless, and that if anyone should move this bag, it should be Matt.

Aside from Shoe Mountain, the major moving challenges were the sofas — yes, they had more than one — and the armoire.

Their armoire was 6 feet long and made from solid oak. Lifting it took four of us; we felt like pallbearers. Armoire, by the way, is a French word meaning "is Chef Paul Prudhomme inside this thing or what?"

It would have been easier to put the armoire in an empty field and build a dwelling around it.

Good times can't last forever, though. Seven hours and one McDonald's meal on the kitchen floor after we began, the last crumpled cardboard box and broken lamp were carried into the Encino apartment.

I was beat. My arms hung limply like a puppet's, waiting for my brain to pull the strings to jerk them into action. Simply scratching my back was as complicated as unfolding a canvas deck chair.

In tribute to Henny Youngman, here's a pain-related

joke:

Me: Doctor, it hurts when I do this.

Doctor: Then stop doing that.

In other words, Matt: Never again, pal. Ooooohhh . . .

ᔓ ◈ ᔓ

DOES THE JOB MARKET HAVE YOU AT THE END OF YOUR ROPE?

March 22, 1998

So I was feeling at the end of my rope the other day when — talk about coincidences — I noticed a great job and lifestyle opportunity opening up in Swaziland, Africa, in the form of a "help wanted" ad for a hangman.

That's right, a hangman.

This isn't a joke. The tiny African country is close to executing its first death-row inmate in 15 years. And there's no one to work the rope.

Talk about your knotty problems.

Where's the 1983-era hangman? No one seems to know. Some say he mysteriously disappeared. Others say he went back to his native South Africa. A third version has him quitting out of boredom.

Well, his bosses shouldn't have left him hanging.

(Keep reading; I've got more.)

In the 15 years without executions, criminals have been

stacking up on Swaziland's death row like cordwood. So the government plans to stop stringing 'em along and start stringing 'em up.

Needing someone to work the gallows, the Ministry of Justice has posted an opening for a hangman.

Well, technically, not a hangman. A hangperson.

Great: a politically correct executioner.

According to the minister of justice, the job is open to both sexes. What the country needs, he said, is an able-bodied man or woman "who has what it takes" to clear out death row at Matsapha Central Prison.

Are there other qualifications? How is this job being sold? I can only imagine the classified ad:

"HELP WANTED: Are you a morning person? Like seeing new faces & slipping a hood over them? Exciting career awaits. Work outdoors. Fresh air, mostly. Gd pay, bens. Civil service job. Apply to Human Resources."

Also, where do you think they're advertising? In the noosepaper? (Ba-da-boom!)

Apparently there's a lot of interest. Inquiries have come from across southern Africa.

Hmm. With multiple applicants, how will the Ministry of Justice decide who gets the job?

Maybe applicants will have to try out. You know, weigh a victim for the drop, measure out the right length of rope, tie the slipknot and pull the gallows lever all silently, solemnly and without gagging. (Which could be bad, what with wearing that executioner's hood over your head and all.)

The problem: Who would be hung?

The government could use cloth dummies. although that would lack a certain *je ne sais quoi* (French for "coolness"). Obviously, death-row inmates would be off-limits; otherwise, the job of clearing out the prison might be over before a hangman was even hired.

Criminals need a big sendoff. That's the whole point of executions. Otherwise we'd just empty an assault rifle into every cell and be done with it.

So for the tryout victims, they'd need folks no one would miss. I'm thinking lawyers. Who's going to miss 20 or 30 lawyers, more or less? Even their mothers would breathe a sigh of relief.

If the tryout doesn't produce a clear winner, maybe the personal interviews would. For instance, someone might turn out to be a big fan of swing music.

I plan to try out for the hangman's job myself. Maybe I shouldn't stick my neck out, but I think I have a good chance.

Admittedly, I don't have any practical, on-the-job experience — does anyone? — but I'm eager to learn and I consider myself a quick study. I'm sure that in no time, with a little guidance, I could get the hang of it.

Heck, it sounds like a snap. Of course, the job does have some drawbacks. Details about the country's executioner, including his or her identity, would be state secrets. It'd be like a *Men in Black* deal.

"If you are the hangman, no one wants to get close to you," a government official was quoted as saying. "You have no friends. It is a lonely job."

Do they want a hangman or a Maytag repairman?

Anyway, I've put in my application and resume. (Reference: Dr. Kevorkian.) So far I haven't heard anything.

But my feeling is, no noose is good noose.

TODAY'S TOPIC: BABY GOES TO THE DENTIST

April 26, 1998

No, this isn't a sugary sweet essay about a cute widdle infant's dental checkup. This is a no-holds-barred essay about a squeamish adult's dental checkup.

The baby is me.

Dentists aren't so bad, but let's be honest: A visit to the dentist is about as much fun as an audit.

There's no such thing as a painless trip to the dentist, just like there's no such thing as tasty rice cakes. Discomfort comes with the territory.

So you're always on edge when you go the dentist. I know I was a couple of weeks ago when I showed up to my first checkup since moving to the Inland Valley a year ago.

Who knew what my new dentist would find?

"Sorry, Mr. Allen," she might say, "but we need to do some major work in there. Think you can adjust to a life of eating through a straw?"

Probably because of fears like this, dentist offices employ abnormally cheerful people. The ones in my office smile so much they make the Joker seem like a mope.

The message they're trying to send: "The dentist's office is fun! Fun! Ha ha!"

The message they're actually sending: "We've been in the back, taking hits off the laughing gas!"

Soon I was led down the corridor to the La-Z-Boy Reclining Dental Chair, the one with the overhead lamp, the Li'l Spitter sink and the swing-around tray. Everything but chips.

Heck, there was even a TV, the purpose of which did not become clear until later. (Cue the ominous music.)

Naturally they needed X-rays of all my teeth. Dentists are always taking X-rays. I'm thinking they all invest heavily in plutonium. To prepare me, the dental assistant laid the heavy, silvery X-ray smock on me. I looked ready to umpire a Little League game at Three Mile Island.

Then she stuck those oblong pieces of plastic in my mouth at uncomfortable angles, asked me to bite, aimed a Flash Gordon-type gun at my jaw, zipped out of the room and zapped me. Again and again and again.

Perfectly safe, you say. Uh-huh. If it's so safe, then why does the dental assistant leave the room?

The hygienist worked on me next. She put the pink paper bib on me, making sure that, to meet American Dental Association guidelines, the cold metal necklace lay against the back of my neck.

Then she sat down to stick her fingers in my mouth and scrape my teeth with a series of tiny, sharp hooks until I bled.

What's her name, Hannabelle Lecter?

Once a sufficient amount of my blood had been shed, the hygienist left and the dentist herself entered. And turned on the TV.

She waved a wand around in my mouth. The wand has a teensy security-style camera. The image from my mouth popped up on the TV.

My teeth were magnified so that each one took up most of the screen.

They looked awful. One molar resembled a shiny, mottled mollusk, quivering in its pink shell.

Needless to say: Ick. Is this my personal, private mouth or the Discovery Channel?

My dentist informed me I needed some cavities filled and some old fillings replaced. Whatever you say, doc! Just turn off that camera!

Now it's days later and I'm back in the chair. The dentist brings out the big needle to get me sufficiently numbed to all sensation — a Michael Bolton CD would've sufficed — and moves in with the drill.

For most of an hour I'm lying there helplessly while my mouth contains the following: the saliva hook, the water-and-air jet, the drill, the mirror, the dental assistant's right and left hands and the dentist's right and left hands.

It's like one of those pranks to see how many college students can fit into a Volkswagen. My mouth is the Volkswagen.

"How are you doing, David?" the dentist asks.

"Nngghh," I reply. Don't know about you, but I was always taught not to talk with my mouth full.

Every once in a while she tells me to open wider. My mouth is already open so wide you could slide a whole pie in there. But I strain to crank it open another couple of millimeters.

In real life I rarely open my mouth. Here they won't let me shut it.

I must be bleeding because the assistant is shooting in a blast of water, followed by a blast of air. Water drops spray onto my glasses.

My eyes are as wide as my mouth, telegraphing a silent scream. I'm trying to be brave. Do they give out lollipops to brave adults?

Above the soft whine of the drill and the whooshes of the air and the water and saliva, I hear the wailing of a young child in the next room. The poor kid is apparently being examined — either that, or roasted on a spit.

Good lord.

Where are all those smiling faces when I need them?

'DA BOMB' TAKES ON A WHOLE NEW MEANING IN CHINO

May 24, 1998

So didja hear how some adults, clueless about youth slang, evacuated an entire school in Chino, then blew up a suspicious backpack, all because they didn't understand the slang word scrawled on the pack?

Ha ha! Memo to Clueless Adults: Although you may be unfamiliar with how young people talk these days, let me assure you that there's nothing dangerous or subversive about the expression "23 Skidoo."

OK, OK, Uncle Dave is pulling your leg. (Stop pulling, Mr. Allen, you're hurting us.)

The word on the backpack actually was "Bomb."

Now, police and school officials didn't read this and think: "Slang for 'cool, great, best.' " They thought: "Explosive device, clearly labeled."

So, last Monday, they sent 950 students home, established a 500-foot perimeter "kill zone" around the school and blew up the backpack, which turned out to contain nothing more threatening than crayons and a copy of *Old Yeller*.

Yes, it would be easy to poke fun here, but I think we should sympathize with the adults, once we've finished laughing so hard that our internal organs vibrate.

What if everyone had ignored the backpack, it really had been a bomb and the blast took out a wing of the school? Our reporter would have sternly asked any surviving administrators: "What part of 'bomb' didn't you understand, you morons?"

On the other hand, it's also true that you never saw Ted Kaczynski helpfully writing "Bomb" on his packages. Bombers aren't typically that thoughtful.

Adults who don't understand kids? At its heart, this miscommunication between the generations is nothing new — except for the crater it left on the school yard, that is.

Many, many readers have asked me, "Dave — can we call you Dave? — as the writer who's down with what's up, could you give us the 411 on this 'bomb' slang?"

Gee, how can I refuse when you ask so nicely?

Seeking information like Ken Starr seeks bimbos, I called up Judy Sanders, whose Cal Poly Pomona communications class last year compiled a slang dictionary titled "Da Bomb!"

Right off the bat, Judy had a question.

"Don't the police X-ray things before they blow them up?" she wondered.

Look, Judy, we've moved past that. Try to keep up.

Anyway, "da bomb" means "the best, the greatest, the coolest," she said. "While not as popular as it was last year, it's still a very popularly used slang."

How does she know? Her students eavesdrop on conversations among their peers, using high-tech listening devices known as "ears," then submit the slang terms they hear.

Popular sayings they've documented: "bank," meaning cash; "tight," meaning good; "player," meaning someone who has a lot of boyfriends or girlfriends; and "daveallen," meaning rugged sex appeal. (Shhh! Maybe it'll catch on.)

Judy said "da bomb" exploded (sorry) into the public consciousness because of the 1995 movie *Clueless*. In one scene, a male student shaves his head, his girlfriend makes fun of him and he responds that the look is you-know-what.

Pam Munro, a UCLA linguistics professor who studies slang on the campus, said the expression was probably coined in California, where most bitchin' slang originates (this is not a direct quote).

So how did kids come to say "da bomb" as a compliment? "I wouldn't look for anything very profound. It seems pretty obviously metaphorical," the professor told me. "If something's a bomb, it goes off, it draws your attention to it."

Pam said "da bomb" is an expression "known by everybody" ... everybody outside Chino, anyway. And it's still the most popular slang at UCLA. She's visiting classes and asking students to write down three slang expressions they know. Half the class writes "da bomb."

"Definitely 'da bomb' is the biggest," she said.

Speaking of bombs, that ends another column.

Raise the Curtain for the Not-So-Great Films of the Century

June 21, 1998

Last week, the American Film Institute unveiled its list of the 100 greatest movies of the century — the pinnacle of the cinematic art.

Kept secret, though, were the not-quite-great: films no. 101 to 110. Secret, that is, until an inside source known only as Deep Sprocket leaked them exclusively to this columnist.

The envelope, please ...

No. 101: *Citizen Kane 2: The Reckoning* (1943)

Raised zombie-like from the dead by the evil mystic Chandu, Charles Foster Kane stalks the Earth seeking revenge against his shrewish wife Susan, his traitorous newspaper crony Jedediah, the dirt-digging newsreel reporter and, most especially, the unnamed guy who incinerated his sled. Written and directed by Joe "Slappy" Welles.

No. 102: *Zero Recall* (1996)

Bill Murray stars in this poignant sci-fi/medical drama about a man who keeps reliving Groundhog Day, yet is so forgetful he doesn't realize it. Groundhog (played by Arnold Schwarzenegger) utters film's signature line: "I'll be back."

No. 103: *Swept for You* (1934)

Reserved housekeeper Fred Astaire and fun-loving maid Ginger Rogers squabble over how to dust but agree on how to cut the rug. In a classic scene, a lovestruck Astaire expresses his joy by dancing with a Dirt Devil vacuum cleaner. (Later made into a commercial.)

No. 104: *A Young Woman and the Beach* (1957)

Literary adaptation of Ernest Hemingway's *The Old Man and the Sea*, lightly altered for the big screen. Bikini-clad Gwendolyn's (Grace Kelly) determination to marry an Ivy League man is shaken by a rough-hewn fisherman named Marlin (Tab Hunter).

No. 105: *Bringing Up Bugsy* (1938)

In a botched bank heist, robber Ernie "Bugsy" Buggoli (James Cagney) kidnaps two customers, inept sociologist (Cary Grant) and his spitfire assistant (Katharine Hepburn). Bugsy quickly regrets his choice of hostages after they drive him nuts with questions about his childhood to learn why he turned to crime. Launched brief trend of screwball gangster films.

No. 106: *Eat Lead, My Sweet* (1947)

Film noir classic. Suspected by police in her wealthy husband's decapitation, Theta McVamp (Veronica Lake) hires gumshoe Ace Diamond (Dick Powell) to find the real killer.

Soon Ace is lured into a tangled web of deceit, treachery and hard-bitten double entendres. Classic line: "Actually, that is a gun in my pocket, sweetheart. Now eat lead."

No. 107: *The Day the Earth Moved* (1954)

Sci-fi love story in which the robot Gort (*The Day the Earth Stood Still*) returns to Earth to woo Patricia Neal. Neal tries to rebuff his advances by intoning: "Klaatu barada ixnay on the ooway."

No. 108: *Wiseguys and Dolls* (1988)

Martin Scorsese wrote and directed this madcap musical about the underworld. Robert DeNiro and Liza Minnelli star as the hitman and the hat-check girl who loves him. Signature song: "You and Da Missus Will Be Sleeping With Fishes." Tuneful, bloody.

No. 109: *A Day in Casablanca* (1944)

The problems of three crazy Marx Brothers don't amount to a hill of beans compared to the doomed love affair between Rick and Ilsa, who has returned to Casablanca because she forgot to pick up her dry cleaning.

No. 110: *Unwashed* (1975)

Clint Eastwood stars as the Man With No Hygiene in this unique suspense-Western directed by Alfred Hitchcock. Theft of Eastwood's poncho culminates in a trademark Hitchcock scene of almost unbearable tension: a cat-and-mouse game in an electric fan store between the knife-wielding thief and an unwashed, stinking Eastwood, who tries to stay downwind. Note: Famous for NOT having a shower scene.

Now who'll believe his big scoops?

June 24, 1998

As if you didn't have enough reason to assume everything I write is an irresponsible lie, along comes the news that a newspaper columnist in Boston was fired for making stuff up.

The timing is unfortunate, given that I was putting the finishing touches on my exclusive interview with Elvis.

The King isn't really dead. He's selling novelty license-plate frames from a cart in Ontario Mills.

"Ahwannatellya," he told me, "ah shore like the Inland Valley. Less pressure here. A man can feel at ease."

Wiping his sweaty face with a scarf and tossing it to a bewildered bystander, Elvis confided that he was abducted in 1977 by space aliens seeking his recipe for fried peanut butter and banana sandwiches.

To cover their tracks, the aliens left behind a doppelganger (German for "fake Elvis"), who lies buried at Graceland.

So what's Elvis been doing since 1977? Wandering, mostly. He remembers finding work in Iowa as a Walmart greeter. As a joke, he once entered an Elvis impersonators' contest in Pahrump, Nevada. He finished fifth in a field of eight.

Other than that, Elvis said, the past 21 years are pretty much a blur. (I envy him.)

Before saying goodbye, I bought a license-plate frame with the motto "Honk if You Believe Everything You Read."

"Thankyaverramuch," Elvis said.

Normally I'd be excited by a big scoop like this. But it's tainted, thanks to that Boston Globe columnist.

Patricia Smith — at least, she SAYS that's her name — almost won a Pulitzer this year for her gritty, dramatic columns. Then her editors started checking out her sources and quotes.

Turns out she'd invented more stuff than Thomas Edison.

This makes all us columnists look bad. I'm an ethical journalist. I'm not perfect, but I try to get the facts right. Now who's going to believe anything I write?

In despair, I called up my good friend Madonna.

"Dave, forget Patricia Smith. I'm sure your readers have faith in you," Madonna told me reassuringly.

Madonna always knows what to say.

Thus emboldened, I ran out to chase another hot tip: a mad scientist in Upland who claims to have reversed the effects of aging.

The door was ajar when I arrived at his lab. "Dr. Nutt!" I called out. "Are you here?"

Amidst all the beakers and strange, green liquids running through glass tubing, I found a note.

"Mr. Allen, I'm writing this while I still can," the note read. "My 79 years have been melting away since I took my potion this morning. Yes, my experiment succeeded — perhaps too well."

The stillness was pierced by the cry of a baby, who was sitting on the floor, wearing a white lab coat — and getting smaller by the instant.

"Zowie!" I exclaimed, rushing for the door.

Hours later, another unbelievable story written, I arrived home. But who did I find sitting on my stoop than a forlorn Leonardo DiCaprio.

"Leo, we weren't supposed to get together until Friday!" I scolded him good-naturedly. "What's the matter?"

Leo blurted out his troubles. He'd just been rejected by yet another woman.

This was becoming a pattern with the poor boy.

"I'm trying to stay positive," Leo said, his lower lip quivering, "but I'm starting to wonder if I know how to attract the opposite sex."

I gave him a few quick pointers and sent the grateful lad on his way.

There was one more task before bedtime. I phoned Patricia Smith. I had to ask her: Why? Why did you make stuff up?

Patricia wasn't home, but her dog, Buddy, answered the phone.

Buddy explained that Patricia, crushed by how close she'd come to winning a Pulitzer this spring, stupidly decided to juice up her columns to do better next year.

Now she's unemployed — and probably unemployable.

"Rough," I said. "Rough."

"You took the words right out of my mouth," said her dog.

Scaling New Heights, Not Looking Down

July 22, 1998

Afraid of heights? *Moi*? Yes, *moi*. I can't get close to a ledge without breaking into a sweat. I've never made it higher than the third step of a ladder.

Look down? I even get nauseous looking up. But on a recent Friday, forcing down my fear, I strode manfully into an Upland gym, cinched up a rope harness and scaled a 25-foot wall, using hand- and toeholds the size of soap dishes.

What I won't do for you readers!

The scene was Hangar 18, a climbing gym that just opened in a former citrus-packing warehouse. You climb up simulated rock walls, indoors.

"This is a pretty controlled environment," co-owner Byron Shumpert noted. "You don't have to hike in."

Also: This mountain has air-conditioning! Well, Upland does call itself the City of Gracious Living.

To show me how it's done, 14-year-old Bryan O'Keefe scampered up a rock wall, anchoring the nylon rope on his waist to safety bolts as he went. Pretty soon he was climbing upside down on the rock ceiling.

After reaching the skylight — a feature found on all your better mountains — he slid down.

Bryan, is it hard climbing on the, um, ceiling?

"When you think you're going to fall," Bryan confided, "you get that adrenaline. It really keeps you going."

Heh.

"So, are you ready to climb?" Byron asked me jovially. "We'll get you suited up, sign a waiver ..."

A waiver! Suppressing the urge to direct-dial Johnnie Cochran, I initialed the waiver, promising I wouldn't sue over "any injury to myself or my property or for my death, however caused, arising out of my use of the facilities of Hangar 18 ..."

Gulp.

Thus shielded, Byron handed me my harness and rubber climbing shoes.

Zach Shields, his partner, led me to a wall, then tied a rope from the ceiling to my harness and also to his. This way, he could stay safely on the ground, I could climb up and, if I slipped, I wouldn't fall.

If I did, maybe I'd land on a soft stack of waivers.

"I've never climbed anything before, not even trees as a kid," I warned Zach, hoping to lower his expectations for when I got three feet off the ground and froze.

He assured me I'd be fine. I took a deep breath, placed my right foot on the first outcropping, hoisted myself up — and promptly slid off.

Ha ha. Just kidding, Zach.

Trying again, I gained one hold. Then a second. Then a third. Hey!

"Good!" Zach called up.

Good! Someone thinks I'm good! I wish he'd write a letter to the editor.

Every hold I gained I figured would be my last. But then there'd be another hold right there, so, what the heck, I'd grab it. Amazingly, I looked up and there was the ceiling.

"Touch the top!" Zach said. I did. Then he shouted up how to get down.

Um, what? Did he really say "let go"? My heart was beating faster than a rabbit's.

He repeated: "Just let go, throw your shoulders back and walk down the wall."

In retrospect, I should have made like Batman in the old TV show, walking at a 90-degree angle, talking to character actors who'd stick their heads out of the wall. Instead, I sorta slid down, bouncing.

Nevertheless, I'd climbed 25 feet, which was about 22 feet more than I'd had any right to expect. I felt great!

Then Zach led me to one of the REAL walls.

Turns out I'd been on the bunny slope. On the real wall, the holds are further apart, smaller and harder to reach.

I made it about halfway up, panting, straining, aching. Then my hand slipped. So did the rest of me.

I dangled there in mid-air like a parachutist caught in a tree.

"Do you want to come down now?" Zach called up. "Yes!" I called down.

So I'd definitely recommend you try indoor rock climbing at least once. But personally, next time I climb the walls, I'm going to do it metaphorically.

‘SORRY, WRONG NUMBER’ CALLS ARE PUSHING HIS BUTTONS

July 26, 1998

This is a personal plea to Tom and Dee Monroe: Please, give everyone your new phone number!

Tom and Dee, you see, apparently haven’t given everyone their new phone number. Many people still use their old phone number.

Which is now my phone number.

I’ve gotten so many calls for them, I can mumble “No, the Monroes no longer have this number” in my sleep.

In fact, I think I have.

This has been going on for months. I got my phone number in March 1997, when I moved.

From Day One, there in my new swinging bachelor pad, my phone would ring, I’d answer and the caller would ask for Tom or Dee.

“Um, I don’t know who that is,” I’d say. “I think you have the wrong number.”

Ever notice how we rarely tell people flat-out, "You have the wrong number"? We qualify it: "I think you have the wrong number."

What, is there a chance WE'RE the ones who are wrong? Did we get mixed up on the way home and break into a stranger's house? Could the callers argue with us and convince us that yes, in fact, they DO have the right number?

Imagine my embarrassment if I'd slammed down the phone, feeling smug, then wandered into the spare bedroom and found Tom Monroe there, organizing his sock drawer. "Oh, Tom, you ARE here! Sorry."

But I digress.

(Speaking of digressing, this is as good a place as any to note that I've changed the names in this column to avoid embarrassing anyone. You'll see why in a minute.)

My first thought, when I got these calls, was that the Monroes had been the previous tenants in my apartment, then moved suddenly and left no forwarding number.

Exactly why I thought the phone number ran with the apartment is not clear, although it may be related to the same medical condition (*clueless maximus*) that recently led me to forget the colander and dump my freshly cooked pasta directly down the kitchen drain.

OF COURSE the Monroes did not live in my apartment. They may not even have moved. But they did change their phone number.

And when they did, they must not have asked the phone company for a forwarding message ("The number you are trying to call — blah blah blah blah blah blah blah — has been changed. The new number is ...").

I assumed the spate of calls for the Monroes would be a short-term phenomenon. Surely, people would gradually learn of the Monroes' new number.

Surely, pigs will fly.

Here it is, more than a year later, and I still average two calls a week for the Monroes.

Admittedly, I've probably added to the confusion because the outgoing message on my answering machine doesn't identify me by name:

"Hello, you've reached the city of Rancho Cucamonga Air Quality Hotline! Today looks like another clear, smog-free day in (*cough cough cough hack hack gag*)!"

Well, it cracks up my dentist.

Anyhow, nearly half my messages are for the Monroes. (The implications for my social life are best ignored.)

Because the callers don't realize they've got the wrong number, they sometimes leave elaborate messages.

I've had calls from their insurance agent asking for further information on a claim. From their child's preschool asking for volunteer help. From friends confirming a dinner engagement for that weekend.

Last month, one Monroe friend said he was returning Tom's page. From when, 1996?

The first couple of messages, I returned the calls, even long distance. It seemed rude to let these folks dangle.

Now? I've learned to live with my guilt.

For instance, the other night I found a detailed message from a woman who was calling Dee to get hold of Sylvia — this was a new wrinkle — to go to Monrovia to help at her daughter's home at the last minute.

"It's Tuesday afternoon right now, about — " the woman said, her voice pausing as she looked at a clock, " — 12:30."

Here's what time it is, lady: It's time to get some new friends.

Some people who call are trying to sell the Monroes something. Many sound like they've already sold the Monroes something — and are still waiting for their money.

This may be why the Monroes changed their phone number.

(It's certainly why I changed their names.)

"Mr. Monroe?" the long-distance caller says quickly as I answer the phone. Or even: "Is this Tom?"

"No, they don't have this number anymore," I say.

"Do you have their new number?"

"I don't even know who they are."

They thank me and hang up.

Yet the calls keep coming.

In the phone book, there's a listing for this man under his true name. (It's not with my number, at least.) So, if it's indeed the same guy, he and his wife are still in the area.

Every once in a while, I consider phoning them to ask what their story is.

Like, at 3 in the morning.

ꕥ ◈ ꕥ

FLASH! GAYS RAMPANT; U.S. IN A PANIC!

August 5, 1998

Not to be needlessly provocative, but WHAT, exactly, is the big deal about people being gay?

(Hang on a sec, I can't hear you over the gunfire from alarmed readers.)

So some men love other men and some women love other women. Who cares? Does this affect you personally? How?

Grow up! Can't you leave people alone? Live and let live!!

(Lemme catch my breath while people frantically reload.)

I write these weighty words because of two events in the news.

First, the US. Senate won't fill the ambassador's slot in Luxembourg because the nominee, James Hormel, is (gasp!) gay.

What are we afraid of, that he'll attend a state dinner in Luxembourg and squeeze everyone's thigh? Bob Packwood did the same thing for years and nobody in the Senate cared then.

Luxembourg, big deal. In Monopoly terms, Luxembourg

is the Baltic Avenue of countries. There's probably only four houses and one hotel in the whole place. The main perk is cheap rent.

Some Republicans, though, are pretty worked up about Hormel. "I don't think he represents the majority views of our country," sniffed Sen. Robert Smith, R-New Hampshire.

Is this a new criterion? Look, this is America; the majority of us don't agree on anything, except that movie popcorn costs too much.

A Family Research Council spokesman thundered that Hormel "represents a clear and present danger to our country." Somebody call Tom Clancy!

As if this weren't silly enough, now there are full-page newspaper ads coming out, ha ha, declaring that "Homosexuals Can Change."

Paid for by the Christian Coalition, Center for Reclaiming America and other fun-loving groups, the ads "explain" that homosexuality is a choice — and a pretty crummy one at that.

The groups' goal is to get heterosexuals to convert to homosexuality. Oops, I mean, for homosexuals to convert to heterosexuality. Sorry.

Is this realistic? I know people who stick to one meal, one favorite dish, every time they go out to eat. You expect folks to change their sexuality? You won't even change your restaurant order.

To make their case, these pro-change groups like to cite the example of a former lesbian and a former gay who, in one of life's little mysteries, met, married and had a son.

I figure they met at a party. “You used to be homosexual? Wow, I used to be homosexual, too! Let’s go someplace quiet. There are too many phonies here.”

The ads also thank Trent Lott and Reggie White for their “courage to speak the truth about sexual sin.”

Lott, the Senate GOP leader, compared homosexuality to kleptomania and alcoholism as afflictions that must be overcome. Thank you, Dr. Lott.

White is the former pro football player who called homosexuality “a decision, not a race” and unworthy of civil rights protection. Well, Christianity isn’t a race either, Reg. Should we legalize religious persecution while we’re at it? I mean, while we’ve got the paperwork going and everything.

These ads really go on the offensive — in more ways than one. The homophobe crowd is basically saying, “Hey, WE’RE not the ones with the problem. THEY are. Those homosexuals, over there... Uh-oh, now they’re coming over here. Run!”

Why are some guys so goofy about gays? I lean toward the view of philosopher Jerry Seinfeld:

“I think it’s because, deep down, all men know that we have weak sales resistance. We’re constantly buying shoes that hurt us, pants that don’t fit right. Men think, ‘Obviously, I can be talked into anything.’ ”

It must be tough to be gay, what with people hassling you all the time. (Not that there’s anything right with that.) A funny word, “gay.” Some days, it must seem mighty ironic.

Waiting for a Tow, Time Sure Passes Slow

August 26, 1998

You think it's tough waiting in line an extra minute at the grocery store when some yo-yo ahead of you writes a check?

Try waiting by the side of the freeway, all alone, for a tow truck — for the second time in one afternoon.

Here's how it happened: Headed home one recent Sunday from San Diego, my Toyota Corolla was shaking like a hula dancer with the DTs. Then I heard a pop and saw a piece of my tire whiz past my ear.

Pulling over, I found my front tire was falling apart like a Clinton denial. Great: stranded on the freeway, by myself, on a rural stretch of Interstate 15, late on a Sunday afternoon. All I needed, to make my day complete, was Ken Starr pulling up to drop off a subpoena.

Luckily, a freeway call box was just feet away and help was dispatched.

A tow truck arrived a half-hour later. The driver's shirt was named Kevin. I don't know the driver's name.

He put on my temporary spare and sent me on to Temecula for real help.

Unfortunately, I didn't make it. Within 10 miles, my temporary spare had shredded like coleslaw.

After another roadside call — this was becoming (yawn) routine — I walked off into the bushes to answer a call myself, if you know what I mean.

Then I settled down next to the call box to wait for a tow. It was 5:18 p.m.

The sun was descending toward the mountains. Cars zoomed by a few feet away. Ants crawled up my bare legs.

No one stopped to help. How come there's never a CHP officer around when you actually want one?

(As I later learned, one of those passing vehicles was carrying my colleagues Terry Pierson and Stan Lim, who saw me, debated for 10 minutes whether it was truly me, then lost interest.)

Obviously no mechanics would be on duty by the time I was towed anywhere. I saw a motel in my future.

A little dispirited, I idly wondered if I could use the call box to call my mom and dad to come get me, like when I was a kid and found myself in a place I didn't want to be.

Then I thought, I should use this spare time to reflect on my life. Yessir, take stock. Examine the big picture. Where I stand.

Boy, was that depressing.

Unbidden, the encouraging words of my reader mail came to mind.

Some write to tell me my columns are educational.

"I thought humorists were supposed to be funny. Apparently, I was misinformed," wrote a humbled Michael Lane of Fontana.

Not only does my work offer mental stimulation, I've learned, but certain columns also provoke a physical response.

"Frankly, it made me want to puke!" William L. Prather of Upland reported regarding one of my recent efforts.

And how could I forget the words of Grace Percival of Chino, who was so moved she wrote directly to my boss: "Where did you find such a writer? In my 50 years of taking your paper I have never seen such a waste of space."

It's comforting, in dark moments, to know readers like Grace not only have a sense of history but understand the importance of conserving our dwindling natural resources.

Now what? Maybe singing some cheery Beach Boys songs would lift my spirits.

"'Round, 'round, get around, I get around! Yeah, get around, ooo-ooo-oooh, I get around," I warbled there by the roadside, gazing fondly at my car, which wasn't getting me anywhere.

After "409," "Shut Down" and "Little Deuce Coupe," I had just launched into "Fun Fun Fun" — getting to the part about how she cruises through the hamburger stand now but before the part about how she forgot all about the library like she told her old man now — when the tow truck pulled up at 5:50 p.m.

This one was driven by a man whose shirt was named Cliff.

At least his patch didn't say "Ken Starr."

ꙮ ◈ ꙮ

The Bald Facts on Sheriff's Hair Apparent

September 2, 1998

Last week brought a merciful end to a long-running political coverup.

Clinton? Nah. I'm talking about Lee Baca abandoning his comb-over.

Baca is running for sheriff of Los Angeles County. He makes an issue of Sheriff Sherman Block's health but, sadly, was in denial about his own medical condition, known, technically, as *domius chromius*.

So Baca let what hair he did have grow very, very long, then flipped it over the top of his bald head.

This is supposed to simulate a full head of hair. All of your better car salesmen do it.

Now, this look may have worked well enough when Baca was a low-profile sheriff's commander. Voters took a gander at him, though, and wondered if they should entrust their personal security to a guy who seemed, well, personally insecure.

In other words, his flip-over was a flop. Campaign advisers must have been tearing out their own hair.

So last Friday, Baca showed up to a debate sporting a new haircut.

Courageously, Baca let his hair down. Way down.

He was smooth as an egg.

Block's been that way for years, by the way. So, there in a TV studio, the two of them had a bare-headed face-off over who should be sheriff of Los Angeles County.

It looked like a recruitment session for the Hair Club for Men.

It did NOT look like a casting call for a revival of *Hair*.

(Like Jews telling Jewish jokes, I can safely make these tasteless remarks because Baca and Block are "my people," members of my tribe. Of course, I'm not truly bald. I just have my hair cut this way.)

The debate supposedly showed a new Baca, in more ways than one. Last time, Baca was so timid he couldn't even offer a reason why he should be elected. This time, he came out swinging.

Baca's campaign consultant, Jorge Flores, told me Monday that his man "wanted to reinvigorate himself." Hence the haircut and aggressiveness.

Flores was polite but, understandably, preferred not to talk about the sensitive subject of his boss' newfound resemblance to a bowling ball.

"It's amazing what makes the news," Flores sighed.

Hey, what do you want me to write about, the current worldwide economic collapse? This haircut business is news, baby!

Why? Because, frankly, it's refreshing to see a politician with nothing to hide.

In fact, you could go over both candidates with a fine-toothed comb and not find much.

Whether Baca's skin-is-in look will have the desired effect is up to voters. But it couldn't hurt.

I showed the photo of the old Baca around. His hair was compared to a big yarmulke, a pile of kelp and a frayed rug.

"He probably thought he was fooling everybody," one guy opined. "He wasn't fooling anybody."

My bald friend Tom, who used to do the flip-over himself before giving up, said fooling other people isn't the idea.

"You're fooling yourself," he said sagely. "You're trying to convince yourself, 'See, I still have hair.'

"Once you start flipping over, though, it's hard to give it up. But after one too many windy days, you decide it's not working anymore."

Tom applauds Baca for giving his comb-over the brush-off. Me too.

Now that the matter has been laid bare, it's up to voters: Who's better, Baca or Block?

I predict Baca — by a hair.

The book sequel to *Casablanca* was inspiring cries of desecration when I decided to turn the news into a column. Predictably, perhaps, the book seemed to barely exist outside the hype — I'm not sure I ever laid eyes on a copy — but it did provide a chance to pay tribute to my favorite movie. A co-worker told me this was my first good column because it was about something I actually cared about, a back-handed compliment that rankled because there was a lot of truth in it.

Don't play it again, Sam – please, don't

October 14, 1998

One of the hands-down best movie endings, ever, comes in *Casablanca* when Humphrey Bogart says, "Louie, I think this is the beginning of a beautiful friendship," as he and Claude Rains walk into the fog.

People sometimes wonder: What happens next? The answer's obvious: The words "The End" come up.

Oh, you mean after that? I've never thought much about it, even though *Casablanca* is my favorite movie of all time, and probably yours, too. The story ends on just the right note.

Oops, apparently not.

A brand-new novel picks up the story after the 1942 movie. The title: *As Time Goes By*. (It was either that or *Casablanca 2: The Desecration*.)

We can't pretend to be shocked — shocked! — that the sanctity of a classic like *Casablanca* doesn't amount to a hill of beans in this crazy world.

But of all the beloved fictional worlds in all of cinema in all the world, why did they have to walk all over this one?

Oh yeah — because *Gone With the Wind* was already taken.

So what does *As Time Goes By* say happened next? I refuse to read the book, but based on a newspaper story, which I did read, here are the dopey details:

Rick Blaine, Louis Renault and Sam the piano player escape to Lisbon. They join up with Victor Laszlo and Ilsa Lund in London.

Leaving Sam behind, the foursome get involved in a plot to assassinate a Nazi leader in Czechoslovakia. Louis and Victor die. Ilsa and Rick marry — yes, marry — and return to Casablanca.

I assume they follow this up by having a baby, then take turns saying, "Here's looking at you, kid."

Rick and Ilsa married? Hello? Did someone miss the entire point of *Casablanca*?

You must remember this: Ilsa, Rick and Victor are on the airport tarmac. Only two of them can leave Casablanca. Ilsa is ready to fly out with Rick. Rick tells her she's leaving with Victor, her husband.

"If that plane leaves the ground and you're not with him, you'll regret it — maybe not today, maybe not tomorrow, but soon, and for the rest of your life," Rick tells her.

"What about us?" Ilsa asks.

"We'll always have Paris," Rick says.

Casablanca shows a bitter, I-stick-my-neck-out-for-nobody guy swallowing hard, then sacrificing what he wants for what he knows is right.

In *As Time Goes By*, Rick gets to be noble and STILL gets the girl? Talk about having it both ways.

What's worse than telling us what happens after the movie? Telling us what happened before the movie. The sequel does that, too.

One of the neatest things about *Casablanca* is that we know almost nothing of Rick's past.

We know he was born in New York City, that he's 37 years old and that he can't return to America. "The reason is a little vague," a Nazi major admits to Rick, reading from his dossier. In the sequel, Rick was born Yitzik Baline, worked for a mobster during Prohibition, carried on an adulterous love affair with the wife of a senator that ended with both wife and senator dead, then emptied his boss' safe and fled the country.

Um, I prefer "a little vague," thanks.

One reason Rick is such a compelling character is that he's so ambiguous. Pinning him down is like dissecting a live frog to see how it works — you might find out, but the frog dies.

So will the sequel, and the inevitable movie version, kill the original? Nah.

Monday night I watched *Casablanca* on video for the zillionth time and found it just as funny, moving and beautiful as ever.

Because if a kiss is still a kiss, the movie is still the movie. To further quote the song "As Time Goes By": "It's still the same old story, a fight for love and glory ..."

Or, put another way, they can speculate all they want. We'll always have *Casablanca*.

ᔕ ◈ ᔕ

There's a 'Closed' Sign on the California Welcome Center? That's a Fine How-Do-You-Do

December 2, 1998

They always say California isn't friendly to newcomers. Not friendly? Get outta here! (Wait, come back! It's just an expression!)

California is actually quite friendly. Why, when I arrived here by car in June 1986, I was stopped at the California border checkpoint by a nice man in a uniform who had a question for me: "Do you have any fruit?"

A bit taken aback, I replied: "No, I don't. What do you have?"

Sadly, I wasn't presented a gift basket of California-grown oranges and lemons — they must have been out — but I have to say, it was awfully considerate of the People of the State of California to ask.

Still, this gesture seemed a bit, well, low-key for a state

as full of verve as California. I kept expecting a welcoming committee to jump out from behind a palm tree. "Glad to have you, Mr. Allen!" they'd say, pumping my hand. "Would you like to meet the Beach Boys?"

This never happened. California gets newcomers and visitors whether it does anything or not, so why lift a finger?

So, last year, I was surprised and delighted to hear about the opening of the California Welcome Center.

The Welcome Center was — note the ominous verb tense — in a corner of Ontario Mills.

Perhaps a shopping mall seems like an odd place for California to extend the official Golden State "howdy." I always thought it made perfect sense. What screams "California" louder than a mall?

For whatever reason, I never made it to the California Welcome Center. My feeling was, it was too late for a welcome. Yes, I guess I was hiding the hurt behind a sunny smile.

Last week, though, I read that, because the mall needed the space, the California Welcome Center was closing its doors as of Tuesday.

Yanking its welcome mat. Pulling up stakes. Moving with no forwarding address. (My guess: Oregon.)

Imagine: a "Sorry, We're Closed" sign on the California Welcome Center! Oh, the irony.

Anyway, the impending close shocked me out of my denial. Darn it, this was my last chance for an official California welcome!

Monday, I rushed over to the mall to find the Welcome Center. Turns out it was inside something called the

American Wilderness Experience, which, you might be surprised to learn from its outdoorsy theme, is indoors, inside the mall.

What a great state!

Hidden in the back was the California Welcome Center. It had a room all to itself. Not knowing what to expect, I stepped inside.

Secretly I was hoping for a red carpet, a brass band, some dancers, maybe a song.

"WEL-come to Cali-FOR-nia!/We hope you like our STAAAAATE!/We've got stars and cars/Juice and coffee bars/And we're fash-ion-a-bly LAAAAATE!"

But there was no song. No dancers. No red carpet. No chirpy employees to shake my hand, smile warmly and say, "Mr. Allen! We've been waiting for you for years! Welcome to California! Do you need any fruit?"

In point of fact, I was the only living thing in the room.

Here's what was in the California Welcome Center: a Christmas tree, a glass-enclosed tabletop model of the American Wilderness Experience, a display of fliers for an event that had already taken place, illuminated wall ads — including a poster for the movie *Titanic* that boasted: "Now Showing!" — and racks of tourist brochures like you find in motel lobbies.

Yawn.

If the Welcome Center reopens somewhere else — there IS another mall around, isn't there? — we need some imagination. We need a Welcome Center that would give people a real California-style welcome. For instance, you'd walk into the Real California Welcome Center and all the employees would be milling around, talking into cell phones.

At an interactive kiosk, you'd be asked what freeways you took to the Welcome Center and how long it took. The computer would then tell you another way was shorter.

For refreshments, you'd be offered an espresso and a slice of barbecued chicken pizza. And you could get coupons with special deals: free socks with the purchase of sandals (Northern California) or 10 percent off your first face lift (Southern California).

When you announced you were leaving, the staff would say smugly: "You'll be back!"

Whether or not anyone takes me up on the Real California Welcome Center, it'll be too late to help me. I've given up on getting a glad-to-have-you out of California. Heck, I've been here 12 years.

By California standards, I'm now a native.

ꟷ ◈ ꟷ

Don't have a cow, man! Chino jury duty limited to sitting, waiting, preserving democracy

December 16, 1998

So I was called for jury duty in a courthouse located in, of all places, Chino.

As my friend Mike put it: "Chino? What is it, a cattle rustling case?"

I admit, I never knew there was a courthouse in Chino. This may be the best-kept secret in the Inland Valley. (Next to Mount Baldy on a smoggy day.) Maybe they called me to Chino for jury duty because they need the publicity.

Like a quaint 19th century novel, this all started with a letter. I opened the envelope and the San Bernardino County jury commissioner was telling me I had to report on Nov. 23 to Chino. Can't say I liked the news, but at least she cared enough to write.

Anyway, it turns out they needed me Nov. 24 — and gee, it's nice to be needed! — so I drove down to Chino, which has paved roads and everything, to report for duty.

The Chino courthouse is in the Civic Center complex of buildings, which consists of City Hall, the Police Station, the Courthouse and the Bureau of Cow Emissions.

(Just kidding, Chino! We here in Ontario love you! And your agricultural ways! Now could you spray some Glade or something?)

Inside the courthouse I found the Jury Assembly Room. Cement block walls, fluorescent lights, chairs lined up like a classroom, a TV and VCR set up on a cart in front, a magazine rack near the door. Definitely not one of Martha Stewart's finest hours.

There were 20 of us potential jurors. Some passed the time by reading: a woman read a paperback titled *Dear Emily*, a man read a hardcover whose one-word title took up most of the cover: *BRAIN*. One guy was focused intently on his copy of *Us* magazine like it held the secrets of the universe.

Other people stared off into space, using the time to find a few minutes of peace in a hectic day, or, perhaps, simply waiting for an electric shock to restore brainwave activity.

At 1:30 p.m. we got to watch a video, *Cornerstone of Democracy*. In case you haven't seen it during your own jury duty, this inspiring video explains how we were helping to save the republic by taking time off from work to sit in this room for an afternoon.

The main points that stuck with me:

Thomas Jefferson said that being judged by a jury of your peers is more important to democracy than legislating, but not quite as important to democracy as owning your mistress.

Three judges were shown in the video, and, just like in real life, two of them were women.

The credits said the video's "associate project director" was Ira Pilchen, a guy I went to college with.

The video over, I checked out the magazine rack. A *Ladies Home Journal* issue had Goldie Hawn, Bette Midler and Diane Keaton on the cover. Have they made a second movie together? No. The magazine's date was September 1996.

Similarly, the *Newsweek* issue with a close-up of President Clinton's mug had nothing to do with impeachment. The date: Nov. 18, 1996. The headline: "The inside story of his big victory."

I was a little disappointed not to see a *Life* magazine on John Glenn's flight. The one from 1962.

Luckily, I had come prepared with my own magazines, ones actually published during 1998. For the next hour, the room was silent except for a couple of outbursts of laughter from a man sitting a few feet away from me, reading a magazine.

At 2:35 p.m., the judge came in (without his robe) to tell us that all five of his cases had been settled with plea bargains, meaning he didn't need us. (If there was indeed a cattle rustling case, maybe the suspect had been lynched.)

"Under a new law, you don't have to come back for the rest of the year," the judge told us. "Of course, the year is only a few more weeks ..."

We filed toward the door, a few hours older, a few hours wiser. I passed by the laughing man and saw what he'd been reading. It was the *Newsweek* issue on Clinton's big victory.

Latest Megamerger Joins Christmas, Thanksgiving; Deal May Contain Sanity Clause

December 23, 1998

Capping a frenzied year of corporate mergers, Santa Claus announced today that Christmas is merging with Thanksgiving, a move that will create a $2.2 trillion mega-holiday.

Under pressure to produce profits, Claus stunned the financial world with his acquisition of Thanksgiving, rumored at $600 billion.

Wall Street reacted favorably to the news, sending shares of Christmas soaring.

"This is a real win-win for Christmas and Thanksgiving," said Meg Addeal, an analyst for the First Bank of Moolah. "I don't see any downside. Of course, I'm an unfeeling, money-grubbing hack."

Observers said Claus had little choice but to act boldly. As a mom-and-pop business, Claus and his wife, Mrs.

Claus, have found themselves increasingly hard-pressed to compete in today's cutthroat environment.

Adding to Claus' woes, Christmas was facing a hostile takeover bid by New Year's Day. By buying Thanksgiving, Claus should satisfy lenders and maintain his independence — at least for now.

Claus has a non-exclusive global license to the Christmas holiday, encompassing worldwide gift-giving, toymaking and delivery, but excluding spiritual celebrations.

Claus declines to release financial information, believing it unseemly, but *Forbes* put his 1997 business at $1.6 trillion.

However, Claus isn't getting rich — far from it.

Revenue from licensing use of his image, as well as nominal charges for photographs with children in shopping malls, do not make up for his insistence on giving away all the toys produced at his factory, known to industry as "the workshop."

Most years the ink is as red as his famed suit. And recently, impatient stockholders have been demanding that Claus begin showing profits.

Claus, the majority stockholder, took his company public with great reluctance. In 1995, he had to raise capital to fend off a takeover bid by his rival, the Easter Bunny.

Claus had hoped that stockholders would support his efforts to maintain Christmas traditions, including the nonprofit aspect. This view proved naive, especially given the record-shattering profits posted in 1998 by Halloween.

Analysts say the merger of Christmas and Thanksgiving — which still must be approved by regulators — is a masterstroke, a brilliant yet utterly logical way for Claus to wriggle out of his dilemma.

"Thanksgiving will be a cash cow," said Bo Tomline, who tracks holidays for Merrill Lunch. "Claus can pay dividends from Thanksgiving profits — sales of turkeys, pumpkin-themed decorations, high-margin stuffing and the like — while preserving Christmas as a money-loser.

"Frankly," Tomline added, "I didn't think the old boy had it in him."

With Christmas decorations going up earlier each year, Thanksgiving and Christmas are already blurring into one holiday, offering Claus "a universe of opportunities for synergy," Tomline said.

Thanksgiving gift-giving is only one obvious possibility, observers said.

Repercussions of the Christmas-Thanksgiving merger still must be sorted out.

Consumers and celebrants may not see any obvious impacts, except that Thanksgiving decorations will now bear the motto "Proudly Made at the North Pole."

Claus said the holidays will continue to be known by their current names — for the record, "Christmas" and "Thanksgiving" — because of strong name recognition and brand loyalty.

The Thanksgiving variant name "Turkey Day" can continue to be employed by the irreverent, Claus said.

But for business purposes, the joint holidays will have a corporate name: ThanksMas.

With the merger, Claus appears to have staved off immediate calls for his ouster as CEO. However, Claus isn't out of the woods yet.

His insistence upon home delivery of all toys is seen as hopelessly inefficient. Claus could save untold billions of dollars annually by opening regional distribution centers where presents could be claimed, analyst Tomline said.

Some stockholders grumble that, to trim labor costs, Claus' toy-making operations should leave the North Pole and move to Asia or Mexico.

In the meantime, the merger should not result in the layoff of any elves. However, there is a likelihood of increased reliance on temporary pilgrims.

ITEMS!

Those newspaper scribes whose columns are made up of short bits are generally known as items columnists, with Walter Winchell (in New York), Herb Caen (in San Francisco) and Irv Kupcinet (in Chicago) being the most famous practitioners. It's probably not coincidental that they're all dead, as they represented the apex of a long but vanishing tradition: items separated by ellipsis, the legendary, rat-a-tat three dots.

My items aren't that short; they're a paragraph, or a few paragraphs. And my models were more modern and idiosyncratic.

One was the *L.A. Times*' Steve Harvey, who wrote the "Only in L.A." five-day-a-week column of misspelled menu items, oddly juxtaposed signs and the like. He occasionally would pick up one of my items, giving me credit, and the recognition in a major paper was a small thrill. I studied his columns to learn such writing tricks as how to comment dryly on a photo without repeating its message.

The other was the Bullpen Bulletins page of hype and inside gossip in issues of Marvel Comics. Their breezy style, alliteration and chumminess in the 1960s and '70s helped build a community among readers. I tried mimicking the tone, with inconsistent results, and swiped the punchy opening, namely, "Item!" It was as if news of a writer or artist change on *Marvel Team-Up* had just come in via teletype.

I can't say L.M. Boyd's work was a model, but his syndicated items columns, "Footnotes," were hilariously offbeat. My tribute to his retirement is the last column in this book.

None of my items columns was consistent enough to reprint in its entirety. (Many made for painful reading.) But on the following pages, and again on pages 189-193, I've rounded up the better items from this period, figuring this side of my writing should be represented. Original dates of publication are noted.

Because I prefer writing essays, which give me more room to maneuver, I never exclusively wrote items, and I've gone through brief periods when I didn't write them at all. But there are bits of news that wouldn't get in the paper otherwise — say, a local reference in a sitcom, or a mention in a national magazine — and that beg to be memorialized. Or there are sightings, observations, stray scraps of information or reader contributions that are worth collecting as items.

Besides, they can be a kick to write — and to read.

Nov. 30, 1997

MAULING THE MALL DEPT.: Sure, it's a mega-mall, not a human being, but at 1 year old, birthday boy Ontario Mills shares one crucial quality with infants everywhere.

Namely, it's loud.

From the moment you step inside, the Mills is shouting at you.

The doors open and a recorded voice greets you in two languages. As you stroll around inside, TVs overhead play booming rock music videos. Near the food court ATM comes the unexpected sound of a car whooshing by — probably trying to get the hell out of there.

Everything is beeping, moving and writhing. It's like a mall with attention deficit disorder.

Actually, though, I've grown to like the Mills. It has a great record store, a fun food court and an estimated 67,000 movie screens.

But sheesh, do they have to turn the volume knob to 11?

May 17, 1998

NOT A DEEP IMPACT: According to the *L.A. Times*, a Beverly Hills gallery this weekend is auctioning memorabilia related to U.S. space missions, including the keys to six cities — among them New York City and our very own Ontario.

Presumably, the keys were given to returning astronauts. Estimated value: $100 to $150 each.

Ontario officials took the insult of an auction of a ceremonial city key in stride.

"Our mayor is a big space nut," city spokesman George Urch said. "Maybe he'll bid on it."

May 17, 1998

GAMES DEVELOPERS PLAY: Fancy sales jobs by home builders are nothing new. Back in the 1880s, Ontario founder George Chaffey built a huge bronze fountain by the railroad depot. Visitors who pulled into the train station saw the reassuring sight of gushing water here in the desert.

As soon as the train pulled out, the station master would dash to the fountain to shut it off — before any more precious water went down the drain.

June 28, 1998

READERS CORNER: We've been having fun here on Sundays for months now, but my column's expansion to Wednesdays seems to have brought a slew of new readers, some of whom "welcomed me aboard" with bright and cheery words.

"Oh, YOU'RE the gutless wonder who replaced Chris Reed," one reader greeted me when I picked up my ringing phone. "How much money did Rialto City Hall give you to get rid of him? Don't think we don't know! (*click*)"

Yep, the truth is out there, lady. And so are you.

Overall, though, the response was warm — and gratifying.

"I'm going to take a subscription!" one older gent told me enthusiastically.

Great! Heck, at no extra cost, I'll throw in the rest of the newspaper, too.

July 12, 1998

ITEM! Some government officials have skeletons in their closet. This one has Skeltons in his armoire.

Red Skelton art, that is. Upland City Manager Mike Milhiser's office is decorated in clownish style thanks to the late comic.

A large armoire displays rows of collector plates, 25 in all, featuring clown images painted by Skelton. His hobo alter ego, Freddie the Freeloader, cavorts on most of the plates, playing tennis, flying a biplane, surfing a wave.

Museum-like spotlights illuminate each plate like fine art. Framed Skelton paintings of clowns adorn the office walls.

Somewhere in New England, Martha Stewart is shuddering.

Exactly why is Upland's top government official decorating his stately, paneled office in a circus motif?

"In my business, you have to be able to laugh — and laugh at yourself, too," Milhiser says. "It helps keep things in perspective."

Actually, this is his third City Hall office-cum-art gallery in the Inland Valley. The display has followed him from Montclair to Ontario and now to Upland.

The reverse of each plate bears a quote from the comedian. Milhiser's favorite: "Don't take life too seriously because you'll never get out of it alive."

Could be this column's motto, too.

Aug. 30, 1998

ITEM! In his ballot for the *Bulletin's* recent "Best of the Inland Valley" contest, one reader offered this wiseguy answer for "best place to take out-of-town visitors": back to the airport.

Aug. 30, 1998

ITEM! Who says newspapers never print any good news?

We recently reported that an "apocalyptic denomination" known as End Time Prophetic Ministries is seeking rental space in downtown Ontario — and wants a long-term lease.

If they wanted to go month-to-month, then we should worry.

Sept. 13, 1998

ITEM! Didja see the news that the fossil of a whale was found in ... Pomona?

I say it's only a matter of time before a Pomona entrepreneur launches whale-watching tours.

Oct. 28. 1998

ITEM! What was almost as exciting as seeing Dave Barry at Vromans Books in Pasadena? Being recognized while in line to see Dave by a complete stranger.

Yep, *Bulletin* reader Gene Harvey came over to tell me he likes my column.

Only bum note: Gene kicked off the conversation by asking, "Are you Tim Allen?"

Dec. 6, 1998

ITEM! "Of all my 'unusual skills,' I have a talent for humor," the aspiring diplomat wrote in his application to Claremont Men's College in 1969. "It is my ability to laugh and spread laughter to others that allows me to adapt to new environments."

The writer: Robin Williams. (Yes, that Robin Williams.)

In his freshman year as a political science major at Claremont (now Claremont McKenna), Williams was bitten by the acting bug, thereby changing the course of comedy. And the course of politics, too, I guess.

Dec. 6, 1998

ITEM! Doing hard time ... in the La Verne city jail? Actor Christian Slater seems to think his 59 days in the hoosegow make him this generation's Papillon, based on his comments in the Dec. 10 issue of *Rolling Stone*.

"I was a criminal among criminals," Slater says, probably through clenched teeth, in the magazine's story about his drug-induced biting spree (don't ask). Under the pity-me headline "My Night in Hell," Slater summed up his stint of cooking, mopping and car washing in La Verne as "unpleasant. Not fun. It was not cool."

Sorry jail wasn't cool, Christian.

A 1990s GUESSING GAME: IS THIS CLOTHING STORE FOR MEN, WOMEN OR BOTH? (OR NEITHER?)

January 27, 1999

Have you noticed that clothing stores no longer give you any clear signal as to whether they're selling clothes to men or to women?

Maybe it's all the same to the store, but it's a big issue when you're a customer.

Say you're approaching a store. You look for the store name. It's sexually ambiguous. You peer inside. They seem to have clothes.

For you, though, or for the opposite of you?

Maybe you could tell if you saw customers, but at the moment the store is empty. All you have to rely on is the window displays. This is where you must subtly pick up the clue as to whether, if you walk inside, you'll be fine or make a fool of yourself.

The subtle clue is this: Do all the mannequins have

breasts?

If so, women can safely enter. Men should check their watch and then casually wander away. (Although they might want to continue looking at the mannequins a while, depending on how their romantic life is going.)

Even this principle isn't perfect, though.

Some stores now use mannequins that don't resemble human beings. Have you seen these? These mannequins are like huge pipe cleaners, bent so they have arms and legs and maybe a squiggle for a head.

The men and the women mannequins look the same. So you have to look at the clothes to guess whether they are for men or women.

(Good luck.)

Rule of Thumb: If, around the waist, there's a belt the width of a shoelace, or there's a sash, it's women's clothing.

Now, the tough part is if you find both men's and women's clothing in the windows. Because then, if you get up the nerve to walk inside, you have to determine which side of the store to browse in — as well as which clothes you can safely try on without inviting snickers.

God forbid they should just hang signs: "Men," "Women."

They don't even do this for restrooms anymore. They just stick a silhouette on the door and you have to figure out if it's the men's room or the women's room.

And who's the silhouette artist who decided the only physical difference between men and women is that women, instead of thighs, have a pyramid?

Er, but I digress.

Once you've crossed the store's threshold, you pause. Stores are divided into a men's side and a women's side. You have, at most, three seconds to make a choice — left or right?

Quickly scanning the store for hints, your senses are heightened, like a cheetah's.

Fashion Tip: Surefire gender signals this season are pastels and ball caps.

Once you've determined your side of the store, you're safe. There's an invisible line down the middle, dividing the men's side from the women's side.

This is like the invisible line siblings draw down the middle of the back seat of a car to show whose side is whose. Except that in a store, the two sides may really be equal.

Also, in the store, women can ignore the line. Really!

See, women can wear men's clothes — baggy sweatshirts, overalls, even boxer shorts — and look really, really cute. But men — men can only wear men's clothes, except in special cases.

What a, um, drag.

So if women cross over the invisible line, even accidentally, they can say they were shopping for clothes for themselves, or for a boyfriend or husband. And men can't stop them!

Yeah, you could complain to the store manager up front, but he or she would just turn halfway around and tell you to settle down back there.

Could men cross the invisible line? Sure. But let me tell you, nobody is going to believe you were buying clothes for your girlfriend or wife.

Most men won't even shop for themselves. You expect people to believe you were shopping for someone else?

ᔓ ◈ ᔕ

Angry bees are 25 years late, but the 10-year-old boy in all of us still says: Killer!

February 24, 1999

The killer bees have arrived!

And it's about time.

Scared? Not me.

Personally, I am putting out the welcome mat for the killer bees — making sure, of course, to put out the mat slowly and non-aggressively so the bees don't overreact and sting me to death.

Like many guys of my generation, I have been waiting impatiently for the killer bees for 25 years. Around 1974, I bought a trashy exploitation magazine off the newsstand that was devoted entirely to killer bees. (Er, the magazine, not the newsstand.)

This may seem like an odd purchase, but only to those of you who have never been 10-year-old boys.

Let me tell you, when you are 10 years old and a boy, as

I was, there are few things more exciting than laboratory-created super-insects that escape to wreak destruction on a helpless humanity.

It was like a cheesy horror movie come to life!

Best of all, the killer bees were headed right toward me.

You see, as explained in my magazine, the bees slipped out of a Brazilian lab in 1957 and migrated northward through South and Central America, then into Mexico, probably for the food, then toward Texas.

Their relentless approach was shown by a map of Mexico with a big arrow, representing the bees, pointing north.

North? How thrilling!

You see, I lived in Illinois, which is north of Texas, sort of. Once the killer bees hit Texas, it was only a matter of time before they showed up in Illinois.

And once they were in Illinois, maybe — I could only cross my 10-year-old fingers — they would sting my teachers in their eyeballs and school would be canceled for the year.

Bear in mind, my hometown, bucolic Olney, Ill., was celebrated for its shortage of dangerous wildlife, as illustrated by the town motto, "Home of the White Squirrels."

Unlike killer bees, white squirrels posed no threat. I think all they did, as white squirrels, was carry little briefcases and attend Squirrel Rotary meetings.

So the killer bees would definitely have put some pep in Olney.

The magazine predicted the bees would arrive in Texas in, I think, 1976. However, the bees didn't show up in

1976. I believe they did phone to express their regrets, but all anyone could make out was a high-pitched buzzing.

After this, the bees were always said to be on their way, any year now. Every year, a news story would report that the bees were supposed to have arrived by then, had not arrived, but should arrive the next year. It was like a bee version of *Waiting for Godot*, with Vladimir and Estragon played by entomologists. (Sorry, I was trying to impress my readers in Claremont.)

Why had the bees' advance slowed? Why were they hung up in Mexico? My theory is, they got themselves into a bit of trouble.

They didn't mean to stay so long. Every morning they would wake up, vowing to leave town and head north to attack.

But then one bee would offer to buy nectar, and then a mariachi band would start playing in the courtyard, and a pretty local bee would call one of them "honey," and the next thing the killer bees knew, they were waking up in a strange hive with a pounding headache. Not only that, they couldn't find their stripes.

Finally, in 1994, success! The killer bees made it to the California border, where checkpoint inspectors, ever vigilant, asked if they had any fruit.

The 10-year-old in me heard the news and said: Now we're gettin' somewhere! Go bees!

In mid-1998, the bees got to eastern San Bernardino County and started westward. Just last month, government officials declared that Los Angeles County had been "colonized" by killer bees.

I wept with joy.

All I can say is, I'm happy the killer bees got to my neighborhood before I grew up completely. By the way, if any killer bees are reading this, the Teachers Lounge is that way.

$166 MILLION TOO MUCH FOR A PARK? HAH! WHY, RANCHO CUCAMONGA IS AIMING TOO DARN LOW

March 10, 1999

Great news on the on the leisure front!

No, I don't refer to cityhood for Leisure World — although I could, I certainly could. Say what you will, a city made up entirely of retirees is going to be a pacesetter. Or is that a pacemaker?

(First action of the Leisure World City Council: Strongly worded resolution asking their children to call more often.)

What I'm really excited about, though, is leisure news from Rancho Cucamonga.

Rancho wants to build the biggest, grandest, bestest city park around. Its name would be: Central Park.

Hey, they're promising big, they're not promising original.

Our Central Park would be a sprawling 100 acres.

How big is that? Think of it this way: This park would be five times — yes, five times — bigger than a 20-acre park.

Central Park is big in vision, too. The city newsletter, which I get as a city resident, declares that Central Park will not be only Rancho Cucamonga's "crown jewel" but its "cultural hub."

I'm already nostalgic for our current cultural hub, Blockbuster Video.

According to the newsletter, Central Park will contain — take a deep breath — sports fields, a gymnasium, swimming, tennis, a community center, performing arts center, fine arts center, children's theater, lecture hall, museum — (*pant, pant*) — library, central plaza, a performance pavilion with amphitheater seating, a botanical garden interpretive trail and, the capper, two lakes connected by a stream and waterfalls.

Whew.

No wonder Central Park has never been built. Where would they start?

There may be another reason, too, which is that the price is estimated at $166 million.

To build Central Park, city officials say, homeowners would have to pony up, at minimum, $899 a year for 20 years.

In response, people are giving Central Park a Bronx cheer. (Well, someone had to say it.) As one task force member put it in a recent news story, "Nine hundred dollars a year? I don't think so."

What a defeatist attitude!

Whatever happened to our California optimism, our "can do" spirit? The new millennium is no time for timidity!

I say, let's roll up our sleeves, spit on our palms and shake hands with Destiny.

If we want a crown jewel, a cultural hub, then let's go for the gusto.

For starters: Why don't we have an opera house?

You say, "Because we don't have an opera." What are you, a quitter?

First we build the Cucamonga Opera House, then we start the Cucamonga Opera, bearing in mind the popular saying, "If we build it, they will come and put on horned helmets and sing in other languages."

What else do we need?

We need a zoo.

Yes, a zoo. If I want to see a lion and an elephant, I don't want to drive to L.A. I want to drive to Base Line and Milliken, see a lion and elephant, then make it home in time for lunch.

With an opera house and a zoo, plus a domed NFL stadium and a roller coaster and maybe some horsies, we're well on our way to crown jewel status!

We're also well on our way to spending half a billion dollars, or a whopping $3,000 a year per homeowner. But these figures do not concern me. Why not?

Because I am a dreamer. Because I am a man of vision. But, mostly, these figures do not concern me because I am a renter. Hoo-hah!

To sum up, I encourage Rancho Cucamonga to go for broke. Why stop at "reaching for the stars" when you can reach even further? Say, for a black hole.

Feelin' less groovy at 35, as pop culture – Lauryn who? – slips away

March 14, 1999

A few days before the Grammys, my friend Jan, who's 35, demanded to know: "Who is Lauryn Hill? Why haven't I heard of her before?"

Uh, because you're a fogey?

I don't entirely blame Jan for her fogeyness. I can't listen to the radio anymore either, because every song is either an assault on my ears or on my gag reflex. (An icy death in the waters of the North Atlantic is too good for Celine Dion.)

While I haven't heard Lauryn Hill's music, I can congratulate myself for knowing who she is. You know you're out of it when you haven't even heard of the Grammy nominees. Grammys are such a fuddy-duddy award, the voters think Grandpa Jones qualifies as grunge.

Of course, mentioning Grandpa Jones marks me as a fogey, too. So did recent jokes in this space about Euell Gibbons and "Clinton's wheelchair-using attorney, Ironside."

I'm losing touch. My era was the 1970s. Most of what I

know about current popular culture is from reading about it, not from active involvement.

I haven't been on the cutting edge since I was teething.

Today, incidentally, is my birthday. I turn 35.

Boy, do I feel it.

You see, here in the *Bulletin*'s features department, I work with a lot of young women in their 20s. (Men would kill for my job.) I like these women, I really do. But I they make me feel like a dinosaur.

A baby boomer quiz was circulating. My 25-year-old colleague Holly bombed so badly, she could only, with effort, name three of the Beatles.

The Beatles!

Poor George Harrison, a forgotten man. No wonder his guitar gently weeps.

The other day I jokingly repeated the classic line from *Network* about someone being mad as hell and not taking it anymore. I got a blank look.

A publicity photo for a new singer named Monica Mancini prompted me to suggest that maybe she's the daughter of Henry Mancini, the composer.

"That's funny," an editor said. "Someone else was just saying, 'Maybe she's related to Michael Mancini, the character on *Melrose Place*.'"

(Turns out I was right, though. Score one for experience!)

This one happened at dinner recently. I learned that while younger people may know older songs, they don't necessarily understand them.

My twentysomething friend Crystal, who has brown

eyes, told me she wants Van Morrison's "Brown Eyed Girl" played at her wedding.

"It's our song," she said, affectionately patting the hand of her fiance.

"Your song is about breaking up?" I asked, reasonably enough.

Turns out she had no idea what the song is about.

So much for the wedding playlist.

I'm sure I'm not the only thirtysomething who feels this way. The world is moving so quickly that it's harder to keep up, and easier to find yourself out of it — decades before you're so old you put your urologist on speed dial.

No, 35 isn't old, it's just grown up. Unfortunately, I don't feel grown up yet. But I guess I'd better start.

Because the other day, a document I was filling out asked me to indicate my age range. My choice: 25-34 or 35-44.

You see the significance: My 35th birthday was about to take me from being identified with people in their 20s to being identified with people in their 40s.

Ugh. (Note to my friends in their 40s: I AM referring to you.)

Most popular media and advertising is keyed to the 18-to-34 market. As of today, I'm no longer part of the world's most coveted demographic. Me, a young man of 35, an adult already?

"That's right," my friend Monica said sympathetically. "Advertisers won't be trying to sell you hip, cool stuff anymore. They'll be trying to sell you Preparation H."

Oh.

I told this to Charles, who's 43. He said cheerfully, "You

know, they say Preparation H is really good for getting rid of wrinkles."

To quote the younger generation: Let's not even go there.

ജ ◈ ജ

Over the years I've written many times about the Fox Theater in Pomona, but this next column was the first.

I was there twice in early 1999 for *lucha libre* matches, which took place in a temporary ring set up between the stage and the front rows. These were my first visits to the theater, then something of a glorious wreck, with bright green paint slathered on the interior walls in a misguided attempt by a tenant to spruce it up.

A decade later, the Fox was renovated and many interior details restored, and I've spent many happy hours there at concerts or other events. In the years between, I wrote several times about the Fox's history, current state and the reconstruction and reopening. But I'm glad I got to see the Fox in this dark late '90s period. It sparked my love for the old girl.

Oh, and to explain the column's first paragraph: At the time, NFL great Walter Payton was proposing an NFL stadium in Ontario and was looking for investors who never came. Those were the days, too.

Who was that masked man? It could be a wrestler, as lucha libre invades Pomona!

March 31, 1999

Good news on the sporting front! While we still don't have an NFL team in Ontario, another thrill-packed sport has muscled into the Inland Valley.

Yes, we now have wrestling!

Well, perhaps "sport" is an overstatement.

What we have, specifically, is Mexican-style wrestling. Officially, in Spanish, this style is known as *lucha libre,* which translates, roughly, as "even more fake than pro wrestling."

(Actually, it means "free wrestling," which differentiates it from Greco-Roman, or "real," wrestling.)

Basically, *lucha libre* is like the low-budget TV wrestling you don't see anymore, except that these wrestlers wear masks.

Yes, masks. It's part of the act. By wearing a mask, a *lucha libre* wrestler hides his secret identity from the public.

Also, from his poor mother.

Where is this bit of theater taking place? In an actual theater, Pomona's historic Fox.

It's a strange sight, a wrestling ring inside an old movie palace. The effect is a little sad, a little comical. But at least the Fox is open for business again.

The wrestling itself, which takes place every other Sunday, is great fun. I went a couple of weeks ago and, intrigued but confused, returned last weekend with a translator, my friend Monica, to help with the names and such.

As it turns out, the wrestlers' names are as colorful as their costumes.

There was Espacial ("Spaceman"), clad in a blue, Ultraman-style outfit.

And Amenaza Blanca ("White Threat"), who was naked except for white shorts, a white mask, white kneepads and white boots. He looked like he rolled out of bed in his underwear, put on his mask and came down for action.

Leon de la Muerte ("Lion of Death") was in red and gold, like Shazam, and signed autographs for children after his match.

Other wrestlers included Impacto 2000 ("Impact 2000"), El Mixteco ("The Mixteco") and Black Spider ("Black Spider"). Monica, thanks again for translating.

Basically, the wrestlers in bright colors represent the forces of good, while the wrestlers in black represent the forces of evil. The crowd hisses and taunts the villains and roots for the heroes.

The action is just as exaggerated. The wrestlers grapple, flip, toss, kick, choke, karate chop, leap onto and slap — yes, slap — each other until one pretends to lose.

Crowd-pleasing moves include bouncing an opponent off the ropes and then stiff-arming him, or climbing onto the corner pole and leaping onto a foe to knock him to the mat.

Sometimes the leaper does a backflip.

That's about as subtle as it gets.

The blows are obviously fake, but they're nothing compared to the reactions.

Wrestlers hitting the mat on their back will flail their arms and kick their feet, and maybe bounce up and down a few times for effect, like they're being jolted with electricity. Or they'll stagger around, palms pressed to their eyes, as if blinded.

This could be a fallback career for Roberto Benigni.

The best moment I've seen so far was when wrestler Acero Dorado Jr. ("Golden Steel Jr.") (I fear my translator is playing a joke on me) fell out of the ring and into the audience, dusted himself off a few inches from the front row, asked a wide-eyed kid for his Coke, took a sip, handed it back and climbed into the ring, revivified.

It was like that old Coke commercial with Mean Joe Greene and the kid in the locker room. All this scene needed was Golden Steel Jr. tossing the kid a sweat-soaked mask.

The second-best moment? It also involved Golden Steel Jr. rolling out of the ring, except I was in the front row and his black-clad bulk was staggering backward directly toward me.

Conveniently, he plopped into the seat to my left, which, even more conveniently, was unoccupied. He got up without a word.

Too bad.

I wanted to ask him if his mother knows he's doing this.

You know, Mrs. Golden Steel Sr.

Lose your keys? Simple problems turn us into morons

April 25, 1999

The latest scientific research tells us that, when confronted by the unexpected, we begin acting, in medical jargon, like bozos.

Say we can't find our keys. (Readers, in unison: "We can't find our keys.")

How do we respond? We begin oh so sensibly. Our keys must be here somewhere. Perhaps in our pants pocket. Perhaps on our kitchen counter. Perhaps on our dresser.

After a few minutes of unsuccessful searching, we're thinking, calmly, sensibly: Perhaps in the toilet tank. Perhaps on the top shelf of the closet. Perhaps in the dishwasher.

Then we catch ourselves being silly. Ha ha! Surely our keys are in an obvious place! We just overlooked them, that's all.

So we try all the obvious places again. And again.

Lost in a fog, panicked but deluding ourselves that we're acting sensibly, we check the same pants pocket for the third or fourth time. Hello! We're not going to mysteriously find a set of keys in our pocket on the fourth try, unless we're David Copperfield.

Pockets are just not that big, even on those pairs of jeans nowadays that are as big as tents.

Realizing this, we embark on the classic strategy of "retracing our steps." That's fun to say, isn't it? "I'll retrace my steps." It's like being Sherlock Holmes.

Self-importantly, believing our steps are somehow worth the bother of retracing, we retrace our steps. Too bad we don't make black dotted lines on the floor, like in a *Family Circus* panel.

Inevitably, this leads to the "when was the last time we saw our keys" strategy. If we can't remember, we shine a bright light in our face and ask ourselves again. We withhold food and water. Slap ourselves around. Maybe this will refresh your memory, punk!

Yes! Yes, it does! Our keys were in our hand this very morning! We put them down on the counter so we could reach into the refrigerator and — there they are!

We're so happy to see our keys, we forget why we needed them. Let's put them down and think.

Uh-oh. Better retrace our steps ...

Needless to say, Bozo Behavior isn't limited to the Key Scenario. What about the Closed Store Scenario?

If we walk up to a darkened store with a "Closed" sign in the window, we can't accept it.

We try the door. It doesn't open. We rattle the handle a

bit, in case it's stuck. Hmm. We can't understand it. Maybe this store is closed!

Having proven to ourselves that the door is locked, we cup our hands around our eyes and peer through the window. Why? What do we hope to see?

Are we afraid the employees are hiding inside in the dark, playing a prank on us?

"Look at that bozo out there," they're whispering to each other, gasping in hilarity, "thinking we're closed!"

These Bozo Moments have been brought to you by Jack in the Box.

ITEM! Perhaps my recent appearance before Mike Eskew's journalism class at Chaffey College didn't go as well as I'd thought. When the campus newspaper, the Breeze, wrote about my talk, I was described as, ahem, "a self-proclaimed humorist."

Next time I'll bring funnier jokes, I promise!

Jury Duty in Sliding-Door Injury Case Was Trial of the Century, in a Manner of Speaking

May 12, 1999

So I recently served on a jury in Rancho Cucamonga in a personal-injury case involving a woman who walked into a sliding-glass door, bounced off, fell on her butt and sued the homeowner for negligence.

This trial dragged on for six days. As you can imagine, I am thankful it ended.

Because now I am free to talk!

Yes, the story of Juror No. 3 can now be told — in the tabloids, in a bestseller that I will co-write with Andrew Morton (*David's Story*), in an interview on *Larry King Live* and in a major motion picture (*An Uncivil Action*), in which I will be played by — who else? — Brad Pitt.

To whet your appetite, here, in a world exclusive, are excerpts from my trial diary.

Day One: Twelve of us are called to the jury box. We are questioned by the lawyers for the plaintiff (the woman who walked into the door) and the defendant (the woman who owns the door) to determine if we can be impartial.

Many potential jurors are excused at the request of the plaintiff's attorney, after they admit they may have trouble evaluating the evidence fairly because they will be laughing too hard.

I skate through. I'm on a jury! On an exciting, high-profile case!

My excitement, however, is tempered by a feeling of danger when I realize we are not being sequestered.

Day Two: The attorneys present their opening statements and testimony begins.

The plaintiff, whom I'll call Sue (har!), described how she walked into a sliding-glass door that had been rendered invisible by having been cleaned thoroughly just hours earlier.

Note to self: Consider changing movie title to *A Clear and Present Danger.*

Day Three: My fears about not being sequestered are confirmed this morning when, upon entering my bathroom, I find a member of the media lurking there, ready to pounce, a startled expression on his face. Then I realize I am looking into the mirror.

During today's testimony, witnesses describe the gathering on the night in question as a meeting of an investment club named Friends Helping Friends, based around "a pyramid-type investment," the details of which the attorneys do not pursue. This is probably wise as many of the members may have a conflict of interest in that they work in law enforcement.

(At the end of the trial, during our deliberations, one juror suggests the group's name should be changed to Friends Suing Friends.)

Day Four: As witnesses offer conflicting testimony about whether the accident occurred more around 7 p.m. or more around 8 p.m., which would bear on the critical issue of the amount of sunlight around the sliding-glass door, I begin to wonder if perhaps I shouldn't be played by Antonio Banderas.

Day Five: In his dramatic closing argument, the plaintiff's attorney refers at length to a TV special on the Titanic that he watched over the weekend when he was, he admits, "supposed to be working on this case."

Not to be outdone, the defense attorney counters with a relevant anecdote from the Adam Sandler movie *Happy Gilmore* regarding a character who wears a T-shirt with a logo reading "Guns Don't Kill People, I Kill People."

Drawing a hilarious parallel, the attorney quips: "The plaintiff needs a T-shirt that says, 'Sliding Glass Doors Don't Kill People, I Kill People.'" He realizes this makes no sense and corrects himself: "Uh, 'Cause Accidents,' I mean."

He wisely changes the subject before the judge brings out a giant hook to yank him away.

Day Six: Tension is thick in the jury room as we begin our deliberations.

Should we give the plaintiff thousands of dollars for her

injuries, lost wages, and pain and suffering? Or should we send her home empty-handed?

We struggle with our decision for at least several minutes. Mostly we struggle with the difficult legal issue of whether, in a civil case, we can give her the chair.

If You've Got the Time, They've Got the Subscription Offer

May 16, 1999

The other day I got a wonderfully flattering letter. (Obviously it wasn't about my column.)

Jack Haire, who is ONLY the publisher of *Time* magazine, the world's No. 1 news magazine, wrote me a letter.

Wrote ME a letter.

Perhaps sensing that I am a busy man, Jack didn't waste any time getting to the point.

"Dear David Allen," began dear Jack Haire, "Let me be frank. There's only one reason I am writing to you."

An autographed photo, Jack? Certainly. How should I make it out?

"I want you to become a *Time* subscriber."

Oh. Heh.

"Why you?" Jack asked, sensibly enough. "As a publisher, I believe a magazine is only as good as the readers it attracts."

I believe other magazine publishers share your philosophy, Jack. For instance, Larry Flynt.

"Therefore," Jack continued, "it is important to me that we obtain the readership of leading professionals such as yourself."

Whoa. Back up.

In case you were reading too quickly, let me repeat the key phrase: "leading professionals such as yourself."

Leading professionals? Such as me?

I don't know whether to send Jack my money or my résumé.

Think about it: The publisher of *Time*, there in the Time & Life Building, Rockefeller Center, New York, NY 10020, considers me, David Allen, of the *Inland Valley Daily Bulletin*, a "leading professional"!

Who knew Jack even READS my column?

Or is his comment proof he doesn't?

Whatever. Let me bask in the glory here. I mean, no one has ever called me a leading professional before.

Come to think of it, no one has ever called me a professional.

But back to Jack.

"So," Jack continued, "I have authorized our business office to offer you a subscription at the low professional rate of just $39.97 for one year — a savings of $149.03 off the cover price."

I can imagine the conversation.

BUSINESS OFFICE: Jack, we're suggesting a low, low rate for David Allen of just $69.97 a year — a savings of $119.03 off the cover price.

JACK: *(pounding desk)* What?! That price would be an insult to a leading professional like David Allen. Make it $39.97.

BUSINESS OFFICE: Are you authorizing that?

JACK: Yes. Bring me the document. *(to cowering aide)* My signet ring and hot wax!

But wait, there's more.

Jack went on to tell me that if I sign up, I will receive *Time's* Preferred Subscriber Advantage, which means "you'll continue to receive uninterrupted service unless you tell us to stop." Gosh, just like water and electricity!

Of course, I won't just be saving money if I subscribe. I will also be acquiring "an invaluable business tool."

Jack explained that *Time* will keep me abreast of business developments, alert me to changes in government policy and the economy, and keep me in touch with "the mindset of today's consumers." Which, personally, I always assumed was: Buy today, pay tomorrow.

I admit, I'm not sure what Jack is driving at. I'm a newspaper columnist, not a businessman.

I don't need an invaluable business tool. I need better jokes.

Jack ended his epistle by asking me to send in my subscription form. He closed warmly: "I look forward to hearing from you. Sincerely, Jack Haire, publisher."

I admit, I haven't responded. I feel really bad about this, especially after Jack's sincere letter.

I can picture ol' Jack — dear Jack! — there in his office at Rockefeller Center, checking the mail daily with increasing concern, pestering his secretary, "Hasn't David Allen responded YET? I was so looking forward to hearing from him."

Perhaps he's thinking, "I hope I got the right David Allen, the one with Mayflower Movers. THAT guy is a loading professional."

ꕥ ◈ ꕥ

Robert Benchley was a humorist for the *New Yorker* and other publications in the 1920s and '30s, an actor and a member of the famed Algonquin Roundtable.

One of my favorite Benchley essays, "More Work Ahead," was about his ostensible hiring to oversee construction of the Hoover Dam. ("The first thing to do, as I see it, is to find the river. I know in a general way where it is...")

In 1999, my newspaper reported on Ontario's annexation of a huge swath of agricultural land north of Chino and the major development coming.

That reminded me of "More Work Ahead," and it occurred to me that I could, like Benchley, pretend I'd been hired for a similarly grand job for which I would have no qualifications whatsoever. I got to work, not on planning the development, but on paying tribute to the master. (I repeated the experiment four months later in the column on page 169.)

How do we develop the Chino Valley dairyland? First, we tell the cows to moooooove

May 26, 1999

The annexation will expand Ontario's city limits from 39 square miles to 52 as it gobbles up farmland to the delight of developers, anxious to carry out the city's master plan of building 31,000 homes and apartments. — Daily Bulletin, *May 20.*

Shocking news, readers! The job of masterminding the development of the Chino Valley dairyland has fallen to ... hold your breath ... me.

(And when it comes to Chino's dairyland, holding our breath is second nature.)

I admit, when they asked me to carry out the master plan for 13 square miles of undeveloped land that could house 100,000 people, I wasn't sure what to say.

I have a lot on my plate already, what with two hard-hitting newspaper columns a week and a firm commitment for eight hours of shut-eye a night.

Plus, I was still bitter after losing out on the contract to oversee the widening of Interstate 10. That failure had forced me to confront the possibility that leading complex, multimillion-dollar public works projects might not be my bag.

But the dairyland development people would have none of this. "You're the man for the job," they said, in unison.

So here I am.

The first task, it seems to me, is to do something with all the cows.

There are something like 300,000 of them. We could go about our business of building streets and homes and schools and Quik-Marts and hope the cows get the hint and leave — but what if they don't?

Then we'd have 300,000 cows roaming south Ontario. It would be like Bombay.

So I think we're better off tackling the cows, so to speak, before developing the area.

Hmm. Any suggestions?

We could bring in the Serbs, tell them we need to "cleanse" the area of cows, turn our backs and let 'em go to work. Refugee cattle would be streaming out of the Chino Valley in no time. Unfortunately, NATO would probably start bombing, hit the refugees by mistake and turn them into hamburger. Literally.

I'd prefer something non-violent. These cows are content and, call me idealistic, I'd like to keep them that way.

My own suggestion is that we get the cows together, explain the situation honestly and straightforwardly, and ask for their help. If we reach out to them, treat them as partners, perhaps they will "buy in" to a solution.

I don't see why we couldn't give each cow a stipend — say, $100 cash — plus a map of California and a lift to the train station. Encourage them to start a new life somewhere, where the grass is green and the livin' is easy.

What will this do to my budget? That's for the bean counters to worry about. I am a man of vision. I've been given a task and I'm going to carry it out as best I can. After all, they knew what they were getting when they hired me.

OK, we have the cows cleared out — theoretically, I mean. Now what?

I'm a big believer in common sense. And common sense tells me that before we go in to the dairyland, we should let the place air out.

This strategy ought to buy me some time. Frankly, I don't have a clue what to do next. Take roads. We could lay asphalt anywhere on those 13 square miles. Who knows where to put it?

Boy, what a pickle.

Maybe we should start with the housing. They tell me that plans call for 31,000 houses and apartments. That's a daunting number. In fact, whenever I think about it, I feel like quitting. Maybe we should do the housing last.

(My suggested architectural motif for the development, by the way, is Spanish tile. But I'm open to a new approach, like creative use of bamboo.)

The trick will be to take on the housing in bite-sized

chunks. That's the only way to keep our sanity. Because if we go in, build the first house and think, "That took a week and we still have, gulp, 30,999 to go," we'll all get discouraged and begin drinking.

What I'll do is tell the boys their job is to build 31 houses and apartments. Then, when they're done, give them another 31 to do. And so on, until we have 31,000. That's psychology!

I'm already planning my kickoff pep talk to the crew. We'll get them together in the valley, out in the sun.

"The road ahead is long," I'll warn. "Metaphorically, I mean. Technically, there are no roads at all. Your job is to put the roads in. *Capisce?*"

Note to self: Remember to leave room in the town square for a statue of myself!

Class clown? Him? Awful truth revealed

May 30, 1999

Ever get asked a question that really knocks you for a loop?

(Uh, hope I didn't just knock YOU for a loop.)

In my case, I was giving a talk to a classroom of middle schoolers one time, telling them about the glamorous life of a humor columnist (cough, cough), when a girl asked me, hope in her eyes, "When you were in school, were you the class clown?"

The Earth tilted on its axis, everything went fuzzy and when they picked me up off the floor, I could only answer, sadly, "No. I was the class nerd."

It's true. As a child in bucolic Olney, Ill., I was about as close to being class clown as Strom Thurmond is to joining the Backstreet Boys. In fact, classmates voted me Person Most Likely to Never Be Class Clown. No one even thought I had a sense of humor.

All those nasty letters to the editor last year trashing my column? I think they were all written by old schoolmates.

I was considered so non-funny, I was the object of pity. My senior year of high school, a girl took me aside to tell me, kindly: "David, you're a smart boy and you should focus on that. You shouldn't try to be funny. You just embarrass yourself."

(I understand she went on to become a career counselor. She advised Bill Gates that his future lay in musical theater.)

Today I can laugh about not being funny. I could laugh then, too, except no one would laugh with me.

That's why I was so surprised by this middle school girl's question. Even in an alternate reality, I could not have been class clown. I didn't have what it takes.

Basically, I was pigeonholed as the Smart Kid.

But, boy, I would've loved to have been known as the Funny Kid.

I did have potential. From an early age I had a sense of the ridiculous. Being an outsider all through school only heightened it.

Tragically, though, I could only be funny in very small groups, when I felt I could let down my guard and relax. In larger groups, the pressure was too great and I got tongue-tied.

I was WAY too shy for the role of class clown, which demands a willingness — a compulsion, really — to make yourself the center of attention.

I was in awe of the class clowns. Jealous, too.

Take Jeff Van Metre. I had to sit next to him in Mrs. Richardson's journalism class. Jeff was, to be gracious about it, an obnoxious jerk.

But he was a FUNNY obnoxious jerk. Once I was in a fender-bender car accident, in which I'd backed into someone's car. (This gaffe was helpfully reported in the *Olney Daily Mail*'s "Police Log" feature.)

The next day, when I sat down in my chair in class, Jeff spontaneously reenacted the accident by making revving noises with his mouth and scooting his chair backward to ram violently into mine.

See? Obnoxious, but funny.

There was also Donita Polk, a rare example of the female class clown (*femmicus mirthicus*). In English class, during study time, she liked to whisper to the teacher, "Psst! Linda!", causing Mrs. Kowalis to look up out of reflex, then wince because she'd answered to her first name.

And there were the anonymous kids in study hall brave enough to sneak phony pass slips into the pile for Mr. Franklin to read aloud, like for "Dick Hertz." Seventeen years after I graduated, I still find this funny.

So, to circle back, against all odds, to my main point: Nope.

Not me, middle school girl. I was no class clown.

In fact, nobody who knew me back then would have believed this, that one day someone would figure that, OF COURSE, David Allen was the class clown.

Kid, you made my day!

Men! Boys! Pick up women without even breaking a sweat

June 27, 1999

Amscray, femmes! Today's column is for guys only. Guys, gather 'round.

Today's topic: How to pick up women. Most single guys (and some married ones) want to know how to pick up women. The process, to us, seems magical. We can't figure out how it's done. We assume mirrors are involved.

I'm not much help here, I'm afraid. If I were to write a self-help book titled *My Secrets for Picking Up Women*, the sum total of my tips would be as follows:

1. Pick a fairly slim, light woman.
2. Stand behind her and grab her below the ribcage.
3. Heave.

Obviously, *My Secrets for Picking Up Women* would join the ranks of the world's thinnest self-help books, alongside *Diet Tips From Camryn Manheim* and *Bill Clinton's Guide to Monogamy*.

However, I met a guy recently who could write a book on picking up women and make it as thick as a phone book.

His name is Pierre. Seriously.

I'd describe Pierre as an average-looking guy, kinda preppy, kinda dorky. (He claims to like opera. His favorite? *Phantom of the Opera.*)

But he IS smooth. And while I watched, he picked up a reasonably attractive waitress. Except for closing the deal, he didn't even leave his seat.

She wasn't even our waitress!

This astounding demonstration, which I wish had been caught on video so that guys everywhere could study it, took place at a supper club in L.A. where four of us were having dinner.

Like any great magician, Pierre worked his sleight of hand almost invisibly, without his audience quite comprehending what he was doing until the trick was accomplished.

I suspect Pierre's feat started with eye contact. First thing I knew, the waitress had bumped Pierre's elbow as it stuck over the back of the booth. This prompted a short but intense, and friendly, conversation.

A few minutes later, during another of her passes by our table, she initiated a second conversation, even squatting down for the one-on-one. They appeared to again be discussing the elbow incident, an unpromising topic that in their hands had become lively and engaging.

From this point I was rapt. Sitting next to Pierre, I had a ringside seat for his magic show.

Progress, though, pulled a disappearing act for the next

half hour. Pierre looked at the waitress whenever she passed near. She studiously avoided returning his gaze.

Later, as the onstage swing combo swung, she unexpectedly turned up behind Pierre and told him not to mind her, she was just listening to the band. He turned in his seat and stuck out his hand.

"I'm Pierre," he said.

Pierre! She almost floated off the carpeting.

During dessert, she dropped by again. (I think we saw more of her than our own waitress.)

This time, Pierre took her left hand, as a pretense to asking about the ring she wore on her ring finger. He asked playfully, "Is there any special significance to THIS ring on THIS finger?"

The answer was no. They talked a full minute. He held her hand most of that time.

"When you get a chance," he told her firmly, "I'll need you for five minutes."

Not long afterward, she returned. Pierre, for the first time, stood up. He took her aside. They chatted amiably for five minutes.

Pierre returned to our table to get a pen and a piece of paper.

A minute later, slipping the scrap of paper into his pocket, he took his seat, in quiet triumph.

I don't know what lessons that we as guys can learn from this demonstration, other than that it helps, with women, to have a name like Pierre.

For his part, Pierre was modest about his achievement,

so we didn't press him, although we did suggest that he should be leading seminars.

He did give a hint of his method when the conversation turned to the subject of whether it's OK for women to make the first move.

Pierre says sure. Even he can't always tell when women are interested, he admitted. But not knowing, he said, is the risk you take.

"I call it the rocking chair test," he said, in his most philosophical comment of the evening. "Do you want to be 90 years old, sitting in your rocking chair, wondering what would have happened all those years ago if you'd had the nerve to talk to that person?"

Pierre, I suspect, is going to be in that rocking chair at age 90, looking back on a lifetime of risks taken. And smiling like a son of a gun.

Ontario's Street Planters Seem Like a Roundabout Way to Slow Down Speeding Traffic

June 30, 1999

I was going to hem and haw before revealing the topic of today's column, but I decided to tell you in a direct, straightforward manner that it's roundabouts.

Roundabouts, sometimes known as traffic circles, are a quaint, picturesque way of slowing traffic by sticking something right in the middle of the street that you have to go around. No, not like roadkill.

An East Coast phenomenon, like cheesesteaks, egg creams and nasal accents, roundabouts have found only limited success in California. All of a sudden, though, they seem to be Traffic Solution No. 1 in the Inland Valley.

Ontario just plunked down four of 'em on Sixth Street. Claremont plans to stick a couple on Indian Hill Boulevard real soon. They'll join a longstanding roundabout in pioneering Upland (civic motto: "The City of Circuitous Driving"), a big ol' bandstand in the middle of Second Avenue downtown that does a nice job of slowing traffic in a charming way.

Ontario's roundabouts are small round planters with a tree and some flowers. They're getting bad reviews, causing city poobahs to back away from the plan to put in six more.

Needless to say, I had to check out the roundabouts for myself, because I care deeply about engineering advances in the important field of transportation humor.

Sixth Street is a nice little residential neighborhood — individual, unique homes that look to date to the early 1960s — with one lane of traffic in each direction. Unfortunately, the street runs parallel to Interstate 10, which is just to the north, and gets more, and faster, traffic than it should.

I was puttering east on Sixth from Benson Avenue when suddenly, there arose in my path: a tree.

It's a small tree, yes, but it's still a tree, and it's smack-dab in the middle of the street, which is not where you expect to see a tree, unless there's been a strong wind. The planter, such as it is, is maybe five inches high, surrounded by a concrete curb, exactly like a sidewalk curb.

Frankly, this dinky thing isn't much of an obstacle. I watched from the side of the road while drivers going 40 mph jerked their wheel an inch to maneuver around the roundabout without even slowing down.

You'd think they would at least tap their brakes, gape and shout, "What the heck is that?" People are so jaded today.

Sixth has three more roundabouts in a row further east, past San Antonio Avenue, that work better because they're concentrated. They're also marked in advance — mysteriously so. A sign shows a diagram of a dot and two squiggles that looks like something from a football playbook. The sign reads: "Traffic Calming Ahead."

"Traffic Calming"? I didn't even know it was agitated. And how do you calm traffic?

Maybe Ontario should put out loudspeakers to play Yanni, or post a sentry to hand drivers a Prozac. I don't think the roundabouts are soothing anyone.

In my considered opinion as a humor columnist, the roundabouts are a nice idea, but they're just too small to slow traffic or beautify the neighborhood.

My thinking is that roundabouts can work, they just need to be bigger and more eye-catching. Maybe they could be tailored by each community to make an artistic statement.

For instance, in Claremont, a roundabout could be a huge wheel of Brie. In San Dimas, a Conestoga wagon wheel. In Chino, a live cow, mooing and munching grass inside a round wire pen.

Your ideas, readers? Drop me a line about what sort of roundabout would be nice for your city.

Don't beat around the bush — give me your straight views on the roundabout. I'll pile up your replies right in the middle of my desk, so I won't miss 'em.

ಌ ◈ ಌ

If cops and firefighters get own Olympics, give other professions a sporting chance

July 7, 1999

Didja hear the big news in sports? Ontario gets to play host to the 2000 Games!

No, not the Olympics, silly. Those are going to Sydney, Australia, probably because the Australians out-bribed us. All we could offer the International Olympic Committee were bargain-priced silk shirts from Ontario Mills.

(By the way, what, exactly, qualifies Sydney as a world-class, Olympic-worthy city? People there live in huts, call everybody "mate" and wear those hats with the side pinned up. If the Aussies had their way, Olympic events would include boomerang tossing and alligator wrestling.)

No, Ontario isn't getting the 2000 Olympics. We're getting the 2000 Police and Fire Games.

No kidding. In June 2000, up to 10,000 cops and firehose jockeys from all over California are coming to Ontario to compete in 62 athletic events.

Since the Games are like a police and fire Olympics, I'm thinking their symbol might even be the same: five linked circles.

Except they wouldn't be circles. They'd be doughnuts.

Actually, the Games won't be too different from the real thing. Chip Patterson, a Games spokesman, said events will include volleyball, soccer, table tennis, power lifting, wrestling and karate.

What, no Dalmatian-hurling contest? No pepper-spraying face-off? No battle of (non-) wits to see which cop has the least measurable sense of humor?

I could make many, many more hilarious jokes, but I'd still like to get 911 response.

The existence of the Police and Fire Games gives me an idea, though. I don't know why we don't have Olympic-style contests for other professions.

Why not a Political Games? Local elected officials from all over California could attend the Games — at taxpayer expense, natch.

Featured sports could include Glad Handing (an endurance contest in which politicians shake hands until they drop), Power Voting (how many "routine" items can be piled onto one consent calendar for a single vote?) and the Secrecy Sweepstakes (to determine who can be vaguest about the reasons for a closed-session meeting).

I'm also eager to see the Lawyer Games ("void where prohibited by law").

In the Damages Derby, lawyers would take turns to see who could ask for the most money without one of the 12 judges laughing.

For the Creative Alibi Competition, lawyers would come up with the best reason why their client was not fully responsible for his/her actions. (Lawyer to beat: the one who argued last month that a guy who stabbed his wife to death was sleepwalking at the time.)

In the Blather Sweepstakes, an essay contest, lawyers would try to take the most words to say the simplest thing.

Tough events? You bet. Expect to see a lot of "pain and suffering" at the Lawyer Games!

Of course, we need a Journalist Games too.

There'll be thrills a-plenty as journalists from throughout the state compete in the demanding events of Freeloading Freestyle (who can eat the most food at a free news-event buffet?), Question Hurling (speed and volume count; accuracy doesn't) and Conclusion Jumping (judges will use a tape measure to determine distance from the truth).

Cops, firefighters, politicians, lawyers and journalists: Let the Games begin!

In the meantime, I'm going for a doughnut.

Readers offer straight talk on roundabouts, say Police Games no laughing matter

July 21, 1999

Regards, readers! Let's relax with a refreshing dip in the ol' mailbag. Yep, I've been flooded with letters, emails and phone calls on my recent columns on Ontario's roundabouts and the 2000 Police and Fire Games.

The response certainly surprised me! The biggest surprise was that so many readers of this column are still allowed access to telephones and writing implements.

First, let's focus our attention like a laser beam on the roundabouts — y'know, the tree planters in the middle of Sixth Street to slow down cars.

Based on the response from you, the motoring public, I would have to send this message to Ontario City Hall: Tear out the roundabouts immediately because they're a terrible idea! But I would also have to send this message: Put in more roundabouts on Sixth and use them throughout the city, because they're great!

Yes, readers sent mixed signals about the roundabouts. Some love 'em, some hate 'em.

A few of you went so far as to offer ideas for what these new roundabouts should look like.

For instance, Milo Arroyo wants downtown Ontario's new Veterans Memorial obelisk plopped in the middle of the busy intersection of Holt Boulevard and Euclid Avenue as a stately, albeit confusing, roundabout. Such a move could bring Ontario national attention and tourist dollars, he says.

"It may be a little costly," Milo admits, "but what the heck, our city officials blow plenty on their worthless ideas anyway."

That's the kind of "can-do" spirit we need, Milo!

Meanwhile, Cherie DuPertuis came up with a new use for Ontario's controversial series of Euclid Avenue nativity scenes: a string of Christmas-themed roundabouts.

Suggests Cherie: "We could inaugurate the whole thing in, oh, say, December, and then..."

Good idea, Cherie! I have to wonder, though: If a driver smacked into a Wise Man Roundabout, could we use taxpayer money to fix him?

Speaking of wise men, or in my case wiseguys, let's move on to my column on the Police and Fire Games, the public safety Olympics coming to Ontario next summer.

In that column, which is sure to be nominated for a Pulitzer, I poked fun at law enforcement and firefighting, wondering if the Games symbol would be five linked doughnuts. I also made hilarious suggestions for Police and

Fire Games events, such as a Dalmatian-hurling contest, a pepper spray face-off and a "battle of the (non-) wits to see which cop has the least measurable sense of humor."

Judging by the response, competition in the latter category should be intense. Several callers and correspondents expressed indignation that I would kid around about people who hold life-or-death jobs. (None of them has ever made any jokes about President Clinton, I'm sure.)

"My husband was very active in these past Police Olympics and I take GREAT offense at your 'jokes,'" wrote Georgia Carpenter. "These guys and gals have an extremely stressful job — dealing with jerks like you — and it is a great way for them to burn off steam in a healthy way. Shame on you!! Shame on you!! Shame on you!!"

I'm sorry, Georgia, could you repeat that? I wasn't paying attention.

Reader Frank Huddleston was offended by my stereotyping of public safety officers, which he considered unfair and demeaning.

Surprisingly, Frank didn't remark on that column's unfair, demeaning stereotyping of politicians, lawyers and, yes, journalists, all of whom I suggested should have their own Olympic-style games. (My proposed events for the Journalist Games were Conclusion Jumping, Question Hurling and, in honor of our penchant for stuffing our faces with free food at news-event buffets, Freeloading Freestyle.)

Veteran firefighter Mike Fechner, in his stern letter to the editor published Tuesday, wrote that he was "extremely upset" by my column. He presented a list of demands, among them "an immediate retraction."

OK, I'm sorry I said some of you guys don't have a sense of humor!

By contrast, there's no doubt that the Police and Fire Games folks know how to chuckle. The morning the column was published, I got a pink box delivered to my desk with the business card of Games rep Susan Palacios. Inside: a dozen doughnuts.

Once I stopped laughing, I called Susan to compliment her on the best joke anyone has played on me in weeks.

"All press is good press," Susan told me. "I told the guys, any kind of awareness we can raise about this is good."

By the way, the *Bulletin's* journalists had those doughnuts inhaled within five minutes. A new record!

ഗ ◈ ഗ

Shortened Workweek in France Makes Him Bleu

July 25, 1999

Welcome, wage slaves! Here's some shocking labor news from France: The French are going to do less work.

Vraiment! (Literally: No kidding!) The government of France is cutting the official workweek from 39 hours to 35 hours.

This caught me off-guard. I like to think I'm "up" on world events, yet I confess I'd never known the French were overworked.

Really, when you think of hard-working, industrious people, you don't think of the French. They don't put their nose to the grindstone. They put their nose to a wine cork.

In fact, when I heard the French were going to a 35-hour workweek, I thought: Finally, we'll get some work out of them!

Then I found out 35 hours is a decrease.

(Note to any French people reading this: Put down that

croissant and get a job.)

Why is the French government cutting the workweek, you ask? To fight unemployment.

With everyone working fewer hours, the logic goes, companies will hire more people.

Economists question whether this will work. Regular French people — is that an oxymoron? — think the plan is wonderful, *naturellement.*

I flew over to Paris in the *Daily Bulletin* jet to get some authentic French people's reactions.

Pierre Froth, coffeehouse employee: "Ze 39-hour workweek, horrors! My arm, she was zo tired from pumping ze espresso machine. Now, wit ze 35-hour week, I have more energy to pursue lithe young blondes and have indiscriminate sex wit zem. Viva le 35-hour workweek!"

Juliette Louis, waitress/actress: "My high-stress job of providing ze intermittent, rude table service will no longer tragically cut into my side career of acting in pretentious avant-garde films."

Jacques Le Broome, shop employee: "I am glad for ze break from my career of sweeping ze floors of ze quaint Left Bank bookshop while daydreaming of a past that never was and a future that can never be."

Jean-Claude Les Miz, theater set designer: "Now, wit ze extra four hours a week, I can pursue my dream of watching ze *oeuvre* of ze genius filmmaker Jerry Lewis!"

Marie Flour, baker: "*Zut alors!* Staggering into ze boulangerie at ze crack of 10 a.m., I could only mutter 'Time to make ze pastry,' like in ze old American commercials."

So excitement in France is running high. Or at least as

high as you would expect excitement to run in the perpetually bored French.

And why not? They get to work less and — the kicker, or should I say, *le kiquer* — they get paid the same. That's right, 35 hours of work, 39 hours of pay.

(I'm still wondering how the workweek was set at 39 hours to begin with. Did everyone leave an hour early on Friday, or did they all work seven hours and 48 minutes a day? Those wacky frogs.)

My point is, Americans can't get a deal like this. Here in California, all our Legislature will grant us is extra money if we work MORE hours.

Maybe you've heard about this. A new state law will restore overtime pay if you work over eight hours in a day. Last year, the rules were changed so that overtime was paid only if you worked over 40 hours in a week.

How bold. (Yawn.)

Whatever happened to the days of decisive action, of radical change? About the only positive labor innovation of recent years is the 4-10 schedule, in which employees work four hours a day for 10 days, then get four days off.

Dave, you bozo, that's 10 hours of work a day for four days.

Oh. Then they should call it the 10-4. Or maybe the 10-4 Good Buddy.

Anyway, if America is ever going to adopt the French model — and come to think of it, I wouldn't mind adopting a French model — it will take individual acts of courage, such as by newspaper columnists.

Striking a blow for the proletariat, I talked to my boss about changing my working conditions.

"I want to work 35 hours a week and get paid for 40," I announced.

She thought it over.

"We're paying you for 40 now. Why do you want to start working?"

What an Eiffel thing to say.

SALMONELLA-PLAGUED DINING HALL NEEDS FIXING, AND DAVE'S GOT SOME EGGS-CITING PLANS

September 29, 1999

Outbreaks of stomach and intestinal illnesses have got people talking at Pomona College, where at least 122 people have tested positive for salmonella after eating at Frary Dining Hall. — Daily Bulletin, *Sept. 22.*

Thanks for your kind applause, ladies and gentlemen of Frary Dining Hall. I appreciate your warm welcome for me in my new role as your executive chef.

I admit that as a newspaper columnist, I'm an unlikely choice.

"You think salmonella has people talking, wait'll people eat my cooking," were my exact words when they asked me.

But college officials knew what they wanted. They were almost obstinate on that point.

"Dave," they said — for that is my name — "you are the man for the job."

So here I am.

First off, let's concede that we have an image problem.

Image we want to project: Frary is a nice place to get a good meal.

Image we have: Frary serves meals that leave diners doubled over with diarrhea and cramps for four days.

How can we break with the past and get a fresh start? We need a motto.

A few suggestions:

* "Fourteen Proud Days Without an Incidence of Violent Food-Borne Illness"
* "Frary Dining Hall: Catch the Fever!"
* "That's 'Frary' — Not 'Scary'"

Diners need to know they can trust us here at Frary. Frankly, we cannot survive without diners. Luckily, so far, the diners are surviving.

Reform is the watchword. I warn you my administration will bring sweeping changes! Also, mopping changes, wiping changes and food-handling changes.

Let's review the incidents to date.

In July, 29 teen-agers in the Upward Bound program got sick from rotten eggs ... which were downward bound.

Just four days later, 82 people got sick. They were credit union employees. Credit goes to an unsanitary salad bar.

Early in September, at least 11 students got sick, cause unknown.

Regarding rotten eggs, I am going to insist that before cooking eggs, we check the date stamped on the side of the carton. If the date has already passed, we'll give the eggs to charity. Problem solved!

In regards to the salad bar, we have to make sure the hard-boiled egg crumbles don't spill into the diced tomatoes. And we want to wipe up blotches of Thousand Island, ASAP. The little things count!

Also, let's put in a sneeze guard. I'm concerned the current "imaginary sneeze guard" may not be effective.

The Frary menu is another area that's ripe, excuse the expression, for change.

I mean, Thrice-Dipped French Toast on Egg Bread?

We're not serving that on my watch. Ditto with the Unrefrigerated Chicken Salad.

I've heard of sun-dried tomatoes. I am totally cool with sun-dried tomatoes, all right? That said, Pork Left Out in the Sun for Two Days is not a gourmet dish.

We'll also stop serving salmon. I don't know if salmon has anything to do with salmonella, but we don't want to remind anyone of that word.

Any employees here named Sam or Ella? You're fired.

With these crucial changes, I believe we will truly be on our way to creating a "zero-tolerance zone" for gastrointestinal illness here at Frary.

If not? If another crop of diners comes down with salmonella?

Then I'll wash my hands of this job.

Comic Mort Sahl is no longer hip, but as Claremont gig shows, he's still got that edge

November 17, 1999

So, Mort Sahl — did you read about this in the papers? — performed his standup routine in Claremont on Monday.

If you say, "Wow, Mort Sahl!", you're either a cultural historian or old enough to qualify for a senior discount.

Back in the late 1950s and early 1960s, you see, Sahl was a hip young comic, a *Time* coverboy, edgy before the word was invented.

Other comedians wore a suit and tie — I don't think they let women tell jokes onstage back then — and unspooled one-liners about their wife and golf game. Sahl wore a red pullover sweater and carried a folded-up newspaper. He talked conversationally, in pell-mell style, about the issues of the day.

Unfortunately, you can't be young and hip forever. Although I hear science is working on it.

At 72, the shaggy-headed Stahl resembles a clean-shaven Jerry Stiller.

He still wears a red pullover — probably not the same one — and carries a rolled-up paper around like a baton.

He told his audience in Claremont's Cook Athenaeum that he'll begin lecturing at Harvard in February. He thought this was a prestigious appointment. Then he found out the university was playing host to political speaker Warren Beatty.

If Beatty is our leading liberal, Sahl wonders what liberalism means anymore.

"A liberal is someone who believes in abortion, that's about all I can get out of it," Sahl said.

"Conservatives believe in a right to life. But you have to sign a waiver."

Sahl, no surprise, isn't overly impressed by the candidates for president.

On Bill Bradley: "He's aloof. He calls it a Zen quality, because he's afraid you'll interpret it as indifference."

George Bush, when he accepted Christ as his personal savior, said he didn't believe Jews would go to heaven.

A reporter asked, "Wasn't Jesus a Jew?" Bush responded, "I accepted Jesus, I didn't say I accepted anyone who came after him."

Complained Sahl: "George W. Bush is saying they're not making Jews like they used to."

Of Pat Buchanan, Sahl recalled the famous GOP convention speech in which Buchanan rained hellfire and damnation. "I can't help but believe," Sahl deadpanned, "it was stronger in the original German."

He likes John McCain, the ex-POW senator, calling him a real person who believes in something. But maybe, Sahl thinks, "he only wants to be president so he can be a prisoner again."

For a man who describes himself as "basically an anarchist," Sahl seems in surprising sympathy with conservatives.

He said the media have made Gary Bauer, Orrin Hatch and Steve Forbes look like "squares" because "they're not successful liars." And he sees nothing crazy about Ross Perot or the Reform Party.

He scorched Clinton, saying his legacy is that "young people won't aspire to anything."

Are politicians more corrupt today than the 1960s, or does it just seem that way, a student asked.

"I think they're more arrogant today," Sahl said. "They think they can do anything to us."

Afterward, I expressed surprise that he'd spent so much time mocking the left.

Equal opportunity, he told me. Besides, true liberals seem to be in hiding and the Democratic Party has been taken over by moderates.

What's his current political philosophy?

"Lean to the left," he said, "but correct for drift."

At the time the next column was written, I was a general assignment reporter for the *Bulletin* besides writing two columns per week. The city editor — the same one who wrote the foreword to this book! — sent me to Walnut High School on a Monday morning after school district officials told us excitedly that *60 Minutes* was coming.

That turned out to be a bust, and the editor decided there was no story. Which was true. Reluctant to let a morning's work go to waste, though, I turned my notes into a column about the anticipation.

Students wait for their '60 Minutes' of fame at media-besieged Walnut High

November 24, 1999

They were a little nervous Monday morning at Walnut High School. That's understandable, given that at any moment a *60 Minutes* crew was set to arrive.

What was Mike Wallace going to expose — bad cafeteria food?

Not at all. Supposedly, *60 Minutes* was doing a "good news" story — and have those phrases ever appeared together in the same sentence? — on Walnut High as a model of ethnic diversity.

This may be the first time in history that any officials heard *60 Minutes* was coming and reacted by getting EXCITED.

"Well, you always have some apprehension about *60 Minutes*," admitted Principal Ken Gunn. "But the media's always been pretty positive."

True.

In fact, Walnut High is so popular with the media, the school should hire an agent.

The attention started when *National Geographic* printed a photo of the school's mixed-race dance team with a caption that explained: "In 1986, 52 percent of the students were white, 16 percent Asian. Today, 23 percent are white and 52 percent are Asian."

Soon the *L.A. Times* was running a long piece on Walnut High's demographic flip-flop and how well its 2,400 students mix.

For instance, the Asian club has a black president, the black club has a white adviser and, a couple of years ago, the Middle Eastern club had a Jewish adviser — who by now must be a U.S. envoy.

After that story, network TV got interested. In a big way. *60 Minutes II* called, but they wanted an exclusive, which Gunn couldn't promise — not just because Walnut High is a public school, but because ABC and NBC were also calling. *NBC Nightly News* visited a month ago.

On Monday, the anticipated *60 Minutes* drop-in had Walnut Valley Unified School District spokesman Mike Bowers feeling almost giddy as he prepared to leave for Walnut High.

"If *20/20* calls," he joked to secretary Mary Ann Ryono, "you'll have to page me."

Bowers and I waited in the Walnut High lobby for *60 Minutes* to walk in, which is the opposite of how it usually works. You're supposed to walk into your lobby to find *60 Minutes* waiting for you.

Sadly, it wasn't *60 Minutes* that showed up. Maybe Mike Wallace is still recovering from seeing *The Insider*.

Instead, we got *CBS Evening News*. Not Dan Rather, just a producer from New York named Raylena Fields, plus two cameramen from L.A.

They didn't even jump out from behind a bush.

After introductions, the crew dropped into a meeting of the student government cabinet.

"What do you want us to do?" adviser Jim Faren asked.

"Pretend we're not here," Fields said.

So the teenagers tried to go about their business as if nobody was there — not a man with a camera on his shoulder, circling the table, and certainly not a man holding a boom microphone over their heads as they spoke.

Students are becoming media savvy, though.

"So we're up against *NBC Nightly News*," one boy said, pondering the CBS program's competition.

Carol Underberger's journalism class is also getting wise.

"Is Walnut unique?" Fields earnestly asked junior Heidi Lyn, tape rolling.

"I know it's unique," Lyn replied politely, "because of all the attention we're getting."

Earth to Mars: Give back our missing probes!

December 12, 1999

Oops, didn't see you at first. I was rummaging around my desk, looking for our missing Mars lander.

We lost it someplace. NASA's not sure where. It could be here under all this paper. I already found half a Mars bar — does that count?

You heard about the missing Mars Polar Lander, right? It was the week's second-biggest story, right after Krispy Kreme coming to Ontario.

This has been a bad year for our Mars probes. First we lost the Mars Climate Orbiter. That's the mission with the math problems, where some of the engineers were using metric and others used English, or "normal," measurements.

We're not sure what happened to the Climate Orbiter after we launched it, but we think it ended up in Cleveland.

Now we've lost the Polar Lander and its two auxiliary probes. After they got to Mars, we never heard from them.

Hope dims with each passing day, but NASA officials still have their fingers crossed that they'll get a postcard.

We're not sure what to do about all these lost probes. NASA's entire Mars exploration effort for 1999 — price tag $356.8 million — has failed.

Maybe we haven't spent enough. That's what a lot of independent space analysts think. They say NASA is dooming its own missions by cutting too many corners.

I agree. Based on my own analysis, a sharp upward curve in NASA budgets is needed, as follows:

1999 Budget, Failed Mars Probes: $356.8 million

2000 Budget, Failed Mars Probes: $500 million

2001 Budget, Failed Mars Probes: $750 million

Seriously, though, I AM a little surprised at how relatively inexpensive these missions are. I mean, $125 million for a remote-controlled Climate Orbiter? Which we sent to MARS? Which is 470 million miles away?

Sounds cheap to me. I mean, we're spending $1.2 billion on the Foothill Freeway, and that's only going to San Dimas.

The first Mars mission, back in 1976, cost a billion, and we not only landed an unmanned spacecraft, we got actual TV transmission from the Martian surface. Remember? Live, from the Red Planet, it's NASA! Woo-hoo!

Granted, all we got was a picture of a static landscape, flat, dotted with boulders. It wasn't exactly *WWF Smackdown*. But, hey, it was 1976.

Thanks to budget cuts, NASA has had to downsize its expectations. They're working from the official philosophy of, no kidding, "faster, better, cheaper."

Boy, that's a real winner.

Hey, let's save even more money: Instead of launching spacecraft, let's just dump them directly in the ocean. That cuts out an entire step in the process! Talk about efficiency.

Of course, maybe it's not cost-cutting and incompetence that's dooming our Mars missions.

Maybe there's a more sinister explanation.

I mean, don't you think it's a little suspicious? We send up the Mars Climate Orbiter, it enters the Martian atmosphere, we lose it. We send up the Mars Polar Lander, it enters the Martian atmosphere, we lose it. Ditto with the two auxiliary probes.

What if the spacecraft aren't "lost" at all?

What if the Martians, using their advanced alien technology, are SHOOTING OUR SPACECRAFT DOWN?

Really, to the Martians, this has got to look like we're invading their planet. Think about it, people. By now they've seen four of our spacecraft in their skies in just the past few weeks! (Official Martian government explanation: Weather balloons.)

What if the Martians retaliate by launching an invasion force of their own?

We are SO toast.

And after their conquest of Earth, imagine the glee of our Martian overlords as they bring out their fiendish alien torture devices to humiliate us.

"Hey, buddy," they'll say, leering, "we've got your 'Mars probe' RIGHT HERE."

❧ ◈ ❧

As with *Casablanca* earlier in this book, *Peanuts* is something else I care about quite a bit. I've been a fan of comic books and comic strips since boyhood. It's not a subject I've written about often because comics are of interest to only a small subset of the population, the recent superhero movies aside.

Charles Schulz's retirement, soon to be followed by his death, was a chance to write knowledgeably about a comic that everyone knew, and I didn't let it pass.

Rats! 'Peanuts' is ending, and that's one thing you can't be wishy-washy about

December 15, 1999

No more Charlie Brown, no more Snoopy, no more Linus, Lucy, Schroeder and Woodstock?

To quote Charlie Brown: "Aaughh!"

Forgive me for getting sentimental, but I love comic strips and I love *Peanuts* more than almost any of them. Tuesday's news that cartoonist Charles M. Schulz is retiring means the funny pages are going to be a little less funny.

We'll never know if Charlie Brown will get to kick that football — and if you don't understand instantly what that means, where have you been the last 50 years? — or if Linus will give up his security blanket or if Snoopy will succeed in shooting down the Red Baron.

If this is tough on us, think how it must be for Schulz. He's written and drawn *Peanuts* all by himself, every day of every week, since Oct. 2, 1950, never taking a vacation, never running a repeat.

In fact, when he faced heart surgery in 1981, he worked ahead so the strip wouldn't, so to speak, miss a beat.

"You don't work all your life to get to do something so that you can have time NOT to do it," Schulz once said.

He'd planned to continue *Peanuts* until he dropped. Like his alter ego Charlie Brown, Schulz is no quitter. But the 77-year-old Schulz has colon cancer and decided health problems and daily deadlines don't mix. Instead, we'll get repeats. No one else will ever draw "Peanuts." How could they?

So many of its set pieces have entered the national consciousness:

Linus waiting in vain for the Great Pumpkin. Lucy leaning on Schroeder's toy piano. Snoopy sleeping atop his doghouse. (Oh, his aching back.)

Lucy at her psychiatric booth, dispensing advice at the pre-inflation price of a nickel. Snoopy acting out his rich fantasy life as Joe Cool, as the WWI flying ace, as the world-famous surgeon.

Charlie Brown eating lunch alone, pining for the little red-haired girl. Marcie telling Peppermint Patty, "You're weird, sir."

Perhaps because we knew *Peanuts* so well, we took it for granted.

I woke up when a strip a couple of years back began with Snoopy walking on his hind legs to the family mailbox, peering inside, thinking, "Hmm...still no word from my publisher." Schulz's low-key absurdity became so commonplace, people quit noticing.

When *Calvin and Hobbes* and *The Far Side* ended, readers went into mourning. Fine, but those creators burned out after about 10 years each. Schulz only stopped a few weeks into his fifth decade.

True, *Peanuts* peaked creatively in the 1960s. Later, Snoopy and Woodstock stole the focus from the gang, and the strip faltered. Some fans gave up. They've missed Schulz's quiet renaissance of the 1990s.

"*Peanuts* hasn't been funny in years," one colleague declared today. I handed him clippings of a few recent strips. He laughed at each of them.

Why has *Peanuts* endured? Maybe because its world is so small, so focused on little people, whose little foibles and failures are, some days, the biggest thing on the comics page.

This will sound silly, but as I sit here writing a farewell to this comic strip I've read for decades, I keep getting choked up. Sad about a comic?

Lucy would say, "You blockhead!" Probably. But why not be sad?

At its best, *Peanuts* always found gentle comedy in everyday sorrows: unrequited love, loneliness and loss — even if the losses were just baseball games and kites. Somehow, even perpetual loser Charlie Brown never gave up hope. Deep down, it was always GOOD grief.

More ITEMS!

As mentioned earlier, my use of items came and went. Wisely, for long stretches of 1999 and 2000 I abandoned the format until I could do better. With reader contributions being scarce, and my grasp of the local scene still sketchy, what I came up with was often pretty lame, which I tried covering up with a jaunty tone that only made things worse.

But from the rubble of these columns, moans from the heartiest items could be heard. Rescue dogs sniffed them out and we pulled the items to safety. Hail the survivors! The rest have been left buried, and we give them a moment of silence.

Jan. 31, 1999

ITEM! The front page of Monday's *Wall Street Journal* carried a story with a Rancho Cucamonga dateline that focused on the city's Frito-Lay and Mission Foods plants.

"Production is humming at the giant chip plants here, helping making this region the hot spot of California's $1 trillion economy," the *Journal* story began. "Tellingly, though, these facilities are turning out corn chips — not computer chips."

Pretty sad when I'm forced to steal jokes from the *Wall Street Journal.*

Feb. 14, 1999

ITEM! So much for your friendly neighborhood library. The recorded message you hear when you call the Claremont Public Library ends: "Please do not leave messages. We will not answer them."

March 7, 1999

One recent evening, I was walking to my car in a Rancho Cucamonga parking lot, at the corner of Archibald Avenue and Foothill Boulevard, when I glanced across Archibald and beheld a business with a surprising name: Claremont Tattoo. Had I lost my mind? (Er, don't answer until you read further.)

Turns out there's a reason why this business is three cities and one county east of Claremont. The studio started in Claremont but, owner Buddy Tanner told me, got zoned out of existence there in 1993.

"I have a letter from the (Claremont) mayor saying our business 'draws an unsavory crowd,'" Tanner said with a chuckle. So he moved to Cucamonga but kept the Claremont name, because, he explained, "when you relocate, you don't want to lose your clientele."

I wouldn't be surprised if Tanner had another reason for continuing to operate as Claremont Tattoo. Namely, to give Claremont the needle.

March 7, 1999

ITEM! Like Elvis, Claremont is everywhere. Don't believe me? Check the phone book for businesses whose names begin with the word "Claremont."

By my count, 17 of those "Claremont" businesses carry addresses in Pomona, Upland, La Verne, Montclair or Rancho Cucamonga.

Claremont may be small potatoes economically, but it's doing very well with exports.

March 24, 1999

ITEM! Don't Know Much About Geography Dept.: I thought it was funny last year when *Rolling Stone* reported that Mount Baldy was "60 miles south of Los Angeles."

Now I'm concerned, because Andy Duggan's new biography of Claremont McKenna alumnus Robin Williams says Claremont is "some 35 miles north of Los Angeles."

North of L.A.? South of L.A.? I could have sworn our inimitable Inland Valley was east of L.A. (Of course, I've been wrong before.)

Then, as luck would have it, some research turned up an old critique of Kem Nunn's novel *Pomona Queen*. The prestigious *Kirkus Reviews* described the book's setting as "Pomona, south of Los Angeles."

If you're keeping score, that's South 2, North 1. Personally, I'd prefer we were west of L.A. Come August, wouldn't you love a gentle ocean breeze?

June 2, 1999

ITEM! Let's observe a moment of silence for this newspaper's Reader Poll (motto: "This is not a scientific poll"), which is kaput, as of yesterday.

As I look back fondly on past Reader Polls, I would have to say my favorite was on April 5, 1997, when the question "Would you ever resort to cannibalism?" prompted 63 percent of the callers to answer (gulp) "yes."

The moral: If you ask a friend "What's eating you?", don't be surprised if the answer is "A *Bulletin* reader."

Jan. 16, 2000

ITEM! My recent visit to Valle Vista Elementary School in Rancho Cucamonga brought the usual amazed responses from the pee-wee set.

"Are you the reporter?" a youngster asked, clearly awestruck.

Why, yes, I am, I told him, flattered.

Still wide-eyed, he asked: "How come you're bald?"

Nov. 1, 2000

SO LONG, STEVERINO: I'm the wrong generation to have grown up with Steve Allen, but I'm sorry to see him go nonetheless. I fondly remember a TV special of his in the 1970s in which, reprising one of his most famous routines, he provided running commentary to footage of people passing by on a crowded sidewalk. When a man in fringed jacket walked by, Allen quipped: "Must be a member of a fringe group."

FUNNY THING ABOUT THE NEW GAME SHOW CRAZE: RICH IN PRIZES, BUT POOR IN SMARTS

January 12, 2000

Everybody said the questions on *Who Wants to be a Millionaire* are dumb, but I didn't know HOW dumb until I tuned in for the first time Sunday night.

"What traditional Thanksgiving dish," Regis Philbin asked, "is also the name of a country: A) Robin, B) Chicken, C) Turkey or D) Finch?"

"Turkey," the contestant said, rolling his eyes.

"Is that your final answer?" Regis asked gravely.

Yes, *Who Wants to be a Millionaire* — the game show whose no-brainer questions start with its own name — is back!

Millionaire was so popular in two test runs last year on ABC that it's now on permanently. At least until people get bored of the novelty of a big-bucks game show in prime time and move on.

Which may happen even sooner, because there are now clones of *Millionaire* on three other networks — all airing at night, all boasting million-dollar jackpots.

So far we've heard from NBC (*Twenty One*), CBS (*Winning Lines*) and Fox (*Greed*).

I'm thinking PBS is next. Except that to raise the million bucks for the prize, they'll have to stop the action midgame and host a pledge drive.

Since prime-time game shows are now a bonafide phenomenon, over the weekend, risking irreversible brain damage, I watched all four.

Boy, are they dramatic. Sci-fi sets, spooky music, wads of bills waved around. Plus, on *Millionaire* you've got Regis goosing up the tension, no matter how mundane the exchange, with his signature line.

REGIS: What do you do for a living?

CONTESTANT: I'm a claims adjuster.

REGIS: Is that your final answer?

What with easy questions, multiple-choice answers and chances to ask for help, though, where's the drama? Barring stage fright, if you've been awake the past 30 years you oughta clean up.

On *Twenty One* on Sunday, a woman won $100,000 — $100,000! — for knowing that "When it rains, it pours" advertises salt, not sugar, umbrellas or raincoats.

Last fall a guy won a million on *Millionaire* for knowing that the U.S. president who appeared on *Laugh-In* was Nixon.

Whatever happened to questions on the Treaty of Ghent

and the prime minister of Lithuania?

So why aren't we awash in millionaires? Because the only thing dumber than the questions are the contestants.

On *Millionaire* on Sunday, one fellow was stumped on what follows "Duck, Duck" in the name of the children's game — the first, softball, $100 question — and had to poll the audience.

How does this guy get his pants on in the morning?

On *Greed*, a team of four struggled with whether Fuji is a type of apple. They thought Best Buy is a bigger chain than J.C. Penney. And they weren't sure what Elton John remake from 1997 is the biggest-selling song in history.

"'Rocket Man'?" one teammate guessed.

I hope their lovely parting gift was birth control.

So which show is best? I'd have to give the nod to *Winning Lines*, the one Dick Clark hosts.

Because it's the most clever, Dave?

No, silly, because at 30 minutes, it's half as long as the others.

In summer 2015, South Carolina was finally deciding to remove the Confederate flag from its statehouse after a white supremacist killed nine people in a black church in the capital city. At the same time, I was rereading my early columns in preparation for this book and came across the following, from January 2000, on a subject then in the news, the Confederate flag over the South Carolina statehouse.

It was disorienting to find a topic from 15 years earlier back in the news. The old column was suddenly, if depressingly, relevant all over again.

(Incidentally, the line about Robert E. Lee was a barbed comment on a Claremont racial controversy of that year.)

In South Carolina, Enthusiasm for the Defeated Confederate Banner Doesn't Flag

January 26, 2000

Correct me if I'm wrong, but didn't we win the Civil War? The North, I mean. We gave the South a good thrashing. It's in all the history books.

Yet here is South Carolina, in the year 2000, unbowed, flying the Confederate flag over its state capitol, expressing the proud statement: Neener neener neener.

South Carolina, don't make us come down there and kick your butt again!

You've heard about the flag flap, right? South Carolina — official motto: "The Yahoo State" — is in the news for its stubborn refusal to take the Confederate flag down from its statehouse dome.

Who's the governor there, John Rocker?

South Carolina re-hoisted the flag in 1962, ostensibly to mark the hundredth anniversary of the Civil War, but also

— gee, what a coincidence! — during the height of the civil rights movement, when a bunch of darned outsiders were telling them they should be nicer to black people, in the sense of not randomly killing them and dumping their bodies in swamps.

South Carolina is a much better place now, but they're still flying that flag.

This deeply upsets a lot of people, who assume the statehouse must be controlled by a bunch of racist nuts.

Faced once again with America's condemnation, state leaders remain defiant.

Thumbing its nose at critics, the Legislature recently voted Robert E. Lee "employee of the year."

Of course, like any flag, the Confederate banner is nothing but a piece of cloth, so the fight is over what it represents.

Detractors say it's a symbol of racism and slavery. As far as they're concerned, South Carolina might as well be flying a white hood with two eyeholes.

Supporters say the Confederate flag is historic, a symbol of Southern heritage, a reflection of pride and tradition.

You see, the flag conjures up a more genteel time, when folks drank mint juleps, danced at cotillions and relaxed on their porches at sunset, lulled by the sound of their happy workers singing spirituals in the fields, in between beatings.

Unmollified, critics have launched an economic boycott of the state. They intend to cripple South Carolina's vital industries, as soon as they find one.

Further inflaming the issue, presidential candidates campaigning in South Carolina have been pressed for an opinion.

George Bush and John McCain, walking the fine line between self-determination and bigotry, said the state must decide the issue on its own. Then they left to go sit on a fence and eat waffles.

A newly energized Al Gore, meanwhile, has not only condemned South Carolina but offered to parachute onto the statehouse dome and rip the flag to shreds with his bare teeth. Luckily, before Gore could carry out his plan, aides managed to hose him down.

So what's going to happen next?

I suspect the flag isn't long for this world. Apparently there's a lot of sentiment among South Carolina voters to take the flag down.

Unfortunately, there's also sentiment to leave the flag there and, right next to it, mount a gun rack.

Real Rancho Cucamonga not exactly 'Simpatico' with two recent movie portrayals

February 9, 2000

I don't know how your weekend went — get back to me on this — but personally, I spent an enjoyable few hours in Ontario, watching movies set in Rancho Cucamonga.

No kidding! There are two, count 'em, two movies playing right now that take place in Cucamonga: *Next Friday* and *Simpatico*.

Only a couple of scenes of *Simpatico* were filmed here — Ontario International Airport plays itself, as well as doubling for a Kentucky airport — but local references in both movies abound.

"He's probably down at the mall — or he's wrecked the car and hiked to Glendora," Jeff Bridges tells a woman about a mutual friend in *Simpatico*.

But I'm afraid neither movie is going to do much for our tourist trade.

When the San Dimas woman asks Bridges, a wealthy Kentucky businessman, if he grew up around here, he says dismissively, "Just three miles away ... Cucamonga. Pretty boring. 'Home of the Grapes.'"

And in *Next Friday*, a white deliveryman is surprised to find a black man, Ice Cube, answering the door at a ritzy house in Rancho Cucamonga.

"Are you an athlete?" the deliveryman asks.

"Yeah," Cube snarls, "I play for the Cucamonga Cracker Killers."

Ouch.

Actually, while both movies make jokes at our expense, the pictures they paint of Cucamonga aren't all bad.

Just mostly bad.

Simpatico shows Cucamonga as bleak, desolate place that seems to contain only a dive bar called the Fifty/Fifty, a supermarket named the Payless Foods Warehouse and the shack where down-on-his-luck drunk Nick Nolte lives.

"Keep the door locked," Bridges tells Nolte. "It's not safe around here anymore."

Maybe author Sam Shepard — a Mt. San Antonio College alumnus — had his stereo ripped off here once or something?

Still, Bridges' character does retain affection for his weedy boyhood home.

"There's a smell about this place," he tells Nolte's girlfriend. "Alfalfa ... dirt ... a distant, vague smell of alfalfa ... do you smell it?"

Obviously he's sniffing something.

The only weeds in *Next Friday* are smoked, but the movie does at least present Cucamonga as a modern suburbia.

Even though Cube's uncle does mispronounce it as "Rancho CHOOKamonga."

People always have trouble with that name, don't they?

Cube, unimpressed, thinks the town is a "fake-ass *Brady Bunch*" — ouch, again — but despite the slams, *Next Friday* improves on Cucamonga in creative ways.

For instance, the movie invents a downtown Cucamonga — with quaint antique street lamps, no less — which is more than the town fathers ever did.

And spanning the freeway heading into town, there's a nifty metal arch bearing this cheery motto: "Welcome to Rancho Cucamonga, the City Away From the City."

Sometimes, though, the movie's rich fantasy just goes completely over the top.

At one point, Cube's cousin enumerates Cucamonga's charms: "No gunshots, no helicopters, no crack, no gangs — just clean, fresh air!"

Well, it IS a comedy.

Blah Blah Blah Yak Yak Yak

February 13, 2000

Dear Ann Landers: My 16-year-old granddaughter ("Susie") has a cell phone, which she keeps with her 24 hours a day ... Last month, she made 620 calls, and talked for a total of 2,800 minutes! ... We figure this is probably a record. — Proud Grandma in St. Charles, Mo. (letter to Ann Landers, published last Sunday)

Excerpts from the telephone transcripts of Susie:

6:06 a.m.

Tiffany? Susie. Ugh, I can NOT believe I am supposed to get up for school right now. My parents were, like, banging on the door: "Susie! Rise and shine!" like total spastics ... Oh, gawd, here they start again. Peace out.

6:32 a.m.

Tiff, you will totally not guess what my mom is trying to feed me. Blueberry pancakes. I'm like, "Hello? You KNOW I have to have my Frosted Strawberry Pop-Tart in the morning or I am no use to anybody." Then she acts all offended because I don't, quote, appreciate her. Like, it always has to be about her.

8:05 a.m.

Amber? Susie. I have to whisper because I'm in Biology. Jason Tompkins is my lab partner for the dissection. I could die of embarrassment. I can't tell him apart from the frog.

8:17 a.m.

Amber? Jason is waving frog guts at me. I hate him.

9:20 a.m.

Hey, Bill, it's Suz. Whatcha doin'? You're taking a test? OK, I'll hold.

10:48 a.m.

Mom! I told you, NEVER call me during class. I'm trying to study! ... Oh, that's too bad about Dad's accident. He'll still be able to drive me to the mall after school, right? WHAT?!

11:05 a.m.

Steffi, you'll have to drive me to the mall after school. My dopey Dad lost his right hand in the meat slicer at work. They're trying to reattach it, but I don't think it'll be done in time.

11:38 a.m.

Dan? Susie. I'm at the next table. Are you gonna finish those fries?

1:12 p.m.

Hey, Jen, it's Suz. I need your advice DESperately. So I'm in the hall a few minutes ago and that hottie Trent walks by and he's all, "Hey." So I'm like, "Hey." So he's like, "Later." And I'm all, "Sure." Oh, I am SUCH a loser. I can't believe I threw myself at him like that! Can you ask Mandy to ask Jacob to ask around and see if Trent thinks I'm a total slut now?

1:18 p.m.

Hello? What do you mean, Trent doesn't know who I am?!

2:28 p.m.

Steffi, I'll meet you by your car, 'kay? Mall, here we come! I am definitely gonna buy that minidress.

3:12 p.m.

I'm still in the dressing room, Stef. Can you bring me in a size 6? There's something wrong with this stupid size 4.

3:22 p.m.

Um, how about a size 8?

5:15 p.m.

Hello, Mom? Stef and I are at the mall. We're just gonna grab dinner here, OK? Look, don't cry, Mom, I'm sure Dad will be fine. If they can't reattach his hand, maybe they can put in a hook or something ... I'm only trying to cheer you up!

8:43 p.m.

Lesley? Susie. WHAT a day I've had! Trent is totally after me. And I bought a peasant skirt at the mall. That minidress was all wrong for me. Oh, and my Dad had his hand chopped off and successfully reattached through miracle surgery. Thank god. If he had come home with a stump, I would have run away from home, I swear. Your day? Sorry, Les, gotta go.

9:28 p.m.

Hi, Grandma! How are things in St. Charles? You wrote to Ann who? She said I was a compulsive talker? Well! I am speechless! OK, not really. But I'd like to tell HER a few things!

3:41 a.m.

Tiff? I can't sleep.

ꕥ ◈ ꕥ

The backstory to the column you just read came afterward. I mailed the column to Ann Landers with a short, hand-written note, something like this: "Thought you might enjoy seeing this column inspired by one of yours. Best, David Allen."

Imagine my surprise when a business-sized envelope showed up in my mailbox, marked "Personal," and with the return address of Ann Landers. Evidently whoever screened her mail had shown her my column and she liked it enough to respond.

"Your blah-blah-blah, yak-yak-yak column was a hoot. I loved it. Are you syndicated? If not, why not? Please respond to me at the above address. All best, Ann Landers."

The pleasure of this bombshell was only slightly mitigated by her having read my signature as "Daniel" rather than "David."

I wrote her back a few days later, explaining my job and that no, I was not syndicated, but that I would talk to the editor about it, and I enclosed three other columns for her perusal.

It wasn't clear if she had been suggesting she could help or was simply trying to encourage me. I didn't presume anything. I also didn't hear from her again. It's possible nobody showed her my second letter, or that she thought my columns stunk, or that she didn't have any advice or help to offer. But it was awfully nice of her to write the first time.

After all, people wrote TO Ann Landers. I never expected her to write to me.

Ann Landers
Chicago Tribune
435 North Michigan Avenue
Chicago, Illinois 60611

March 30, 2000

Daniel Allen
Inland Valley Daily Bulletin
2041 East Fourth Street
P. O. Box 4000
Ontario, CA 91761

Dear Daniel Allen:

Your blah-blah-blah, yak-yak-yak column was a hoot. I loved it.

Are you syndicated? If not, why not? Please respond to me at the above address.

All best,

Ann Landers

AL:cr

Here's an Umbrella Theory on Why Guys Do Dumb, Manly Things – Like Get Rained On

February 16, 2000

You women think you have it rough? Huh? Do you?

Well, OK, you do. It's probably no piece of cake, being a woman.

But lemme tell you, it's also no picnic being a man. It's certainly no walk in the park, nor is it a day at the beach.

(I've either described the perfect afternoon or set the scene for a feminine hygiene commercial.)

Perhaps you've never considered what guys go through. I don't know how it is with you women and your femininity — get back to me on this — but speaking as a guy, I would have to say that we define our masculinity daily, through a series of tiny choices.

In isolation, these choices appear insignificant, even — yes — silly. Yet when viewed as a whole, in their broader social context, it's obvious these choices are, in reality, completely ridiculous.

Take umbrellas. On Monday I was walking toward Ontario Mills from the parking lot and noticed that, despite the rain, I was the only guy with an umbrella.

Women were carrying umbrellas. That's because women see rain and think, I'd like to be dry, so I'll open this umbrella and walk under it.

Most guys, however, operate under the philosophy that, hey, John Wayne didn't care about staying dry. John Wayne didn't let a little rain bother him.

And so guys brave the elements, just as John Wayne did when he, too, strode resolutely to the mall.

Or how about this: Ever see two guys together in a movie theater — with an empty seat between them?

You don't see women doing this. Many guys, however, need the safety of the Buffer Seat. They may tell you it's more "comfortable," or they need "elbow room." But they're just kidding. Because the Buffer Seat is there to send a message. That message is: "This is not a date! We are just friends! We LOVE women! In fact, ladies, sit here in the Buffer Seat and we'll show you!"

Perhaps along the same lines, guys wrestle with how neat they can be and still seem manly.

This is even true of seemingly well-adjusted celebrities. Check out the covers of magazines. You'll have Jennifer Aniston or Cameron Diaz looking perfectly coiffed. But then you'll have Brad Pitt or Matt Damon unshaven, looking like they styled their hair with a trowel.

ANY outward display of order is considered suspect by guys, most of whom refuse, on moral grounds, to alphabetize their record collection.

Then there's the Diet Dilemma. As guys get older, and thicker, many of us opt for diet soda and lite beer.

But they can be tough to order.

"Diet Coke, please." The words hang in the air. You inwardly wince. You may even see the staff smirk. It's like you just ordered a cool, refreshing glass of Girlie Cola.

So, women, there you have it — a list of just a few of the tough choices facing the other gender. Note: You'll have to put them in order yourself.

Movies, Media Go Cuckoo for Cucamonga

February 20, 2000

Gotta say, I'm disappointed that *Simpatico* and *Next Friday* weren't nominated for any Oscars, such as Best Use of Cucamonga as a Setting.

As you may recall, both films take place largely in Cucamonga, adding to our stock of Inland Valley movie mentions.

For instance, in *Next Friday* the newly relocated Ice Cube is cool to Cucamonga — until catching sight of his lovely next-door neighbor.

"Damn," he mutters, "I'm beginning to LIKE Rancho Cucamonga."

Word!

Likewise, in *Simpatico,* the Kentucky horsebreeder played by Jeff Bridges is initially dismissive of Cucamonga, his boyhood home, when he returns for a visit.

As his personal situation deteriorates, though, his attitude changes. This pivotal, poignant moment is shown in the following exchange between Bridges and his wife, played by Sharon Stone, who has telephoned from Kentucky after not hearing from him in days:

STONE: Lyle, where are you?

BRIDGES: Cucamonga.

STONE: You better get home.

BRIDGES: *(mournfully)* I think I want to stay here.

Those may be Cucamonga's first mentions in the movies, although the town has popped up in other media.

The conductor on Jack Benny's old radio show used to cry out, "All aboard for Anaheim, Azusa and Cuuuuuucamonga!"

Playing off that reference, a Jan and Dean song about a group of hotrodding grannies was titled "The Anaheim, Azusa and Cucamonga Sewing Circle, Book Review and Timing Association."

After singer Johnny Horton had a hit with "The Battle of New Orleans," the novelty act Homer and Jethro responded with a takeoff, "The Battle of Kookamonga."

The Grateful Dead sang "Pride of Cucamonga," while Frank Zappa contributed "Cucamonga," in which he paid tribute to the town where he launched his career.

Rancho Cucamonga has lately made TV, too.

In an episode of *Dharma and Greg*, Dharma opens an "unstore" in San Francisco that sells nothing, prompting her neighbor to suggest franchising the concept to "Fresno, Bakersfield and Rancho Cucamonga."

Somehow I think that was an un-compliment.

Now, columnist Steve Harvey of the *L.A. Times* adds to the list a recent episode of *The Simpsons* that had Homer attending Krusty Clown College.

Krusty tells his students to "memorize these funny names of cities" and holds up cards that include "Walla Walla," "Cucamonga" and "Seattle."

Homer cracks up over Seattle.

D'oh!

An acquaintance at a rival newspaper once said I could get a column out of going for a cup of coffee. I think she meant it as a compliment, although opinions differ. Regardless, in the following example I got a column out of waiting in line at the post office, the sort of commonplace activity that seemed ripe for a Robert Benchleyesque piece of observational humor. Or Seinfeldian, as a reference within the column makes clear. I've never written about getting a cup of coffee, but at least someone believes I could do it.

Time Passing Too Fast? Try Spending It Waiting in Line

March 12, 2000

There's nothing like waiting in line at the post office to disprove the theory that Time always proceeds at the same rate.

Time is more elastic than it's usually given credit for. People ask if you've got "a second," but somehow that second just goes on and on.

People who work hard are said to put in "long hours." How long are those, 80 minutes?

And minutes aren't created equal, either. Some minutes fly by. Conversely, the eminent semanticist and sitcom character George Costanza postulated the existence of "tough minutes," like waiting for the conditioner to set.

Waiting in line somewhere is a succession of tough minutes. You stand, you shift from foot to foot, you day-dream, you people-watch, you occasionally shuffle forward a step or two, and before you know it there's one minute gone.

Last Saturday at the post office, I stood in line with a package to mail for what seemed like, conservatively, forever.

Ahead of me were 10 other people with packages, or with requests too complex to be handled by the stamp machine.

For several minutes the line did not move appreciably. One woman had taken up permanent residency at a teller's station, seemingly intent on requesting one of every service available.

At the other station, a disheveled guy in a flannel jacket had deposited a package boxed so poorly that if the teller had stamped "fragile" on it, the box would have collapsed. She taped it up and gave him some tips for the future, such as, don't use cardboard you find in a catch basin.

Behind me, a college student chatting with her friend emitted a burst of raucous laughter. I turned out of curiosity, accidentally caught her eye, felt embarrassed that I'd looked, then sheepishly turned back around.

Then, progress! Two steps forward.

Opposite me on the wall was a poster illustrating Proper Mailing Techniques. With nothing better to do, I became entranced by the various steps, and especially by the package pictured as an example.

Miss Jane Doe, of 456 Elm Street, Anytown, USA 01234 was listed as the return address on a package going to Mr. John Doe of 123 Oak Street, Apt. 456, Anytown, USA 01234.

Under the bland surface of this poster, a tense drama seemed to be playing itself out. Can't Jane simply drive the package over to John, thus saving the postage? What is the nature of the Does' relationship? Did they break up, badly, causing her to use the mail to return a few small personal effects?

Or am I, yawn, reading too much into this?

Meanwhile, ahead of me, a student in a stocking cap was eating a bagel sandwich and holding a package claim slip. He had a shaved head and was clean-shaven except for a two-inch tuft of blond hair hanging from just under his lower lip. It looked like a snagged string of melted cheese.

Eventually, after what seemed like 45 minutes, I made it to the front of the line. But according to my watch, it had been just 15 minutes.

Fifteen tough minutes.

'TITANIC' STAR'S SUCCESS IN JOURNALISM GIVES COLUMNIST SINKING FEELING

April 12, 2000

So Leonardo DiCaprio, that lovable moppet, actually interviewed Bill Clinton on behalf of ABC News.

Supposedly they talked about the environment. I would love to know DiCaprio's environmental concerns.

"Mr. President," Leo might have asked, brow furrowed, "is the ozone layer affected by hair gel?"

Leo's not really a reporter, he just plays one on TV. He was hired to work on an upcoming Earth Day special by ABC. Coincidentally, the three letters of the alphabet he knows. I'm sorry, do I sound bitter?

And so, on March 31, for the cameras, fellow celebrity Clinton led Leo on a personal tour of the White House's environmentally friendly features.

(For instance, you may not know this, but Al Gore is actually a recycled slab of oak.)

When the tour ended, according to ABC, Bill spontaneously offered Leo a 15-minute one-on-one. The White House begs to differ. They say ABC requested the interview in February, submitted the questions a day in advance and said Leo would be asking them.

Naturally, as a journalist, I am deeply troubled by this situation. Because you're worried about the blurring line between news and entertainment, Dave?

No, silly, I'm worried how I'm going to compete for news against Leo.

Because maybe Leo's interview with Clinton is just the beginning. Maybe he'll decide to stick with journalism as a career.

As a fellow journalist, Leo could be, pardon the expression, a disaster. Ethically? Please. I mean a disaster for me.

If given a choice between A) talking to Leo and B) talking to Dave, you just know everyone is going to pick the world's leading pinup boy. (FYI, that's Leo.)

Sure, my heart will go on — but what about my career? Worried, I asked reporting colleague David Seaton for his assessment. Be frank, I said. Don't spare my feelings.

"Leo's got the star charisma," Seaton said. "He's got the looks. He's got the hair."

Next time, spare my feelings.

There must be some way I can outclass DiCaprio. With reporting, after all, he's on my turf.

"You'll have to rely on your superior intellect, wisdom and experience," Seaton advised. He added: "If it is superior."

Maybe I could talk Leo out of changing careers. I could say, "Leo, bubelah, being a reporter is no day at *The Beach*, ha ha."

Oh, heck.

Maybe I should stop fighting this. If you can't beat him — and lots of people would like to beat Leo — then join him.

What if I mentored him? Took the boy under my wing.

Here's what he gets: the wise observations of a savvy veteran who is at the zenith of his career, here in, um, Ontario.

A few sessions with me, and the next time Leo interviews Clinton, he'll be able to come up with his OWN questions. (Sample: "So, Mr. President! Getting any action?")

I ask nothing in return.

Although Claire Danes' phone number would be nice.

SORRY, PETER: 'JAWS' STILL HAS ITS BITE

April 16, 2000

So, Peter Benchley says he's sorry he ever wrote *Jaws.*

You remember *Jaws.* The bestselling novel by Benchley that became the blockbuster movie by Steven Spielberg.

The movie whose ominous tagline "Just when you thought it was safe to go back in the water ..." became a national catch-phrase.

The movie with the creepy musical motif people STILL imitate to show impending doom: Bom bom bom...bom bom...bom bom bom...bom bom bom bom bom bom BOM BOM BOM BOM (CHOMP) "GAAAAAAHHHH!"

The movie that got everybody scared to go in the ocean, fearful they'd be chomped on by a shark the size of a Pontiac. Ocean, heck — people didn't want to go into swimming pools.

Eat people? Sharks, in Benchley's world, even ate BOATS.

Now he's taking it all back?

Apparently. In the April issue of *National Geographic*, Benchley says that he couldn't in good conscience write *Jaws* today because he's learned that the great white is a misunderstood, fragile and threatened species.

Initial thoughts:

1. Benchley is doing his research 25 years after publication?

2. Will he be personally refunding the $1.50 I spent on a movie ticket in 1974?

3. Does this mean it's safe to go back in the water now?

I still remember the summer of *Jaws.* It was as omnipresent as popular culture got back then. It was the Great White Hype.

Sharks were everywhere. They were in books, on posters, on TV specials, on magazine covers. Shark teeth, real or not, were popular trinkets. I put a shark iron-on transfer on a T-shirt. What can I say, I was 10 years old.

Benchley's novel became a huge bestseller in paperback. Everywhere you went, there it was, with that famous cover art of the naked swimming woman and the equally naked swimming shark rising from below to chomp her in half.

Wow — sex AND death!

(This book was popular on the playground, even. One boy who was allowed to read it brought the book to Silver Street Elementary School and, as we crowded around, showed us the sexy parts. Ooo-la-la!)

Jaws spawned a string of when-animals-attack movies, but don't hold that against it. The movie, justifiably, made Spielberg a star. It's still one of the best movies ever made.

But today, in hindsight, Benchley — the man who put the bom in the bom bom bom bom bom — says he was all wrong about great whites. Oops.

First of all, they aren't terrible killers. They're, ahem, misunderstood.

Is he talking about sharks or Tony Soprano?

And, Benchley says, great whites don't like eating people. In fact, if they bother to take a bite, they spit it out because they don't like how we taste.

Uh-huh. Look, that's nice, but no way do I need a shark casually biting off one of my limbs and then, embarrassed, discreetly hocking it into a napkin.

"Nowadays," writes Benchley, the very soul of tolerance nowadays, "more people are coming to respect and appreciate sharks for what they are: beautiful, graceful, efficient and, above all, integral members of the ocean food chain."

I'm willing to respect and appreciate sharks. But at a respectful, appreciable distance.

Peter, if you're in the mood to apologize for something, apologize for *The Deep*.

Upland City Hall's overspending was news in 2000, and the quote that opens the column, from a news story, seemed like a good launching point for a silly column in which, like an average person, the city goes on a series of shopping sprees that it can't justify.

Afterward, the city manager asked me about the column in genuine puzzlement, asking if the shoes and other items cited were metaphors for various real objects or situations. I told him he was reading too much into it. He said he didn't think the column succeeded as satire, which is possible, although I hope the fabled average person took it as intended.

As I write this in 2016, Upland is still having budget problems, by the way.

Going for Broke, Upland Spares No Expense on Its Way to the Poorhouse

April 19, 2000

At the rate it's spending, Upland is likely to be broke by 2003. "The city has spent more than it's taken in," one critic said. "That's a basic fact of life that any homeowner, any person with a checkbook, understands." — Daily Bulletin, *April 16.*

Future news:

UPLAND, April 20 — Criticism of Upland's spending mounted today when the city arrived home with four new pairs of shoes.

Rather than come through the front door as usual, the city approached stealthily through the back door on tiptoes, Nordstrom shopping bags tucked under its arm.

Taxpayers, who happened to be in the kitchen at the time, busted the city.

"You have a closetful of shoes now that you don't wear!"

they said accusingly.

The city explained sheepishly that it had had a bad day and that shopping gives it "a lift."

UPLAND, April 24 — In a news conference today, the city defended spending $43 on a gross of generic toilet paper at Costco, saying it was too good a deal to pass up.

The bathroom tissue will be stored in Upland's linen closet and used as needed, the city said.

Analysts said the purchase was ill-advised and estimated that the stockpile would last four months. The city brushed off the criticism. "One day, in the middle of the night, you'll thank me," it said.

UPLAND, April 28 — The city today took $64 from a cookie jar and blew it on Russell Stover candies.

The three boxes of $20 "assortments," containing a rich array of creams, caramels, nuts and jelly-filled chocolates, were later found empty under the city's bed.

Confronted with the empty boxes, and a reminder that the cookie jar was specifically there for emergencies, the city said it needed the chocolates because its financial condition left it "depressed."

UPLAND, May 3 — Upland's financial woes continued unabated today as a simple errand at Wal-Mart turned into a $142 shopping spree.

The city intended to buy only a $1.39 Ocello sponge so it could clean the bathroom, sources said.

Two hours later, the city left the store with a cartful of cleaning supplies, snack foods, Diet Coke, underwear and a rake. Eyes glazed, it struggled to explain what it had been thinking.

Taxpayers reacted bitterly upon the city's return.

"We may as well forget about putting in that swimming pool," they said, near tears.

In its defense, the city noted that Wal-Mart boasts everyday low prices and that certain items were discounted further.

"The more you buy, the more you save," the red-faced city said.

UPLAND, May 12 — Finally admitting it has a problem, Upland agreed to attend counseling at Shopaholics Anonymous and to cut up its credit cards. The decision came a week after distraught taxpayers left to stay with their mother "until things get sorted out."

The city hopes to reconcile, promising to be a responsible spender from now on. Starting Monday — after the two-day "white sale."

Central Coast is high on Rancho Cucamonga's Los Osos school name

April 26, 2000

You know how bad this whole Los Osos name flap has gotten? They're making fun of us in, of all places, Morro Bay.

In case you've been in a coma the last six months, let's recap. The name Los Osos was chosen for a new high school in Rancho Cucamonga. This prompted heated complaints from some parents, who say the name is silly.

They don't like the *school's* name, either.

Stop, Dave, you're killing us.

But the school board of the Chaffey Joint Union Rodham Clinton High School District won't budge. Los Osos High School it is. So there the matter lay.

Until now.

You see, up along the Central Coast, there's a TOWN named Los Osos. It's between San Luis Obispo and Morro Bay. And up there, they're laughing at us.

A newspaper columnist, Bill Morem, caught wind of the controversy and wrote a piece about us. (Upland reader Jack Maddux saw Morem's April 5 column in the *Sun Bulletin* and passed it along.)

Under the headline "It's Oso Cucamonga," Morem notes with amusement that some Rancho Cucamonga parents — "the anti-Osans," he calls them — think Los Osos is funny-sounding and prone to derisive nicknames, such as So-So High. If it's such a great name, one parent here asked, "why isn't there a street, housing development or a park named Los Osos?"

Given that its own name has long been the butt of jokes, Cucamonga is probably a little touchy, Morem says. That municipal inferiority complex, he theorizes, may be what led the city "to upscale its name" to Rancho Cucamonga.

He calls that move, ahem, "a vain attempt to emulate all of the faux Spanish-tile eastern San Diego communities that popped up like prairie dogs in the last couple of decades."

"In this context," Morem sniffed, "it doesn't surprise me that Cucamongans would feel more comfort in adopting a name if it had first been appended to a housing development."

Well, I am deeply offended.

Because it was NOT a "vain attempt" at emulating faux Spanish tile communities — it was a successful attempt. As any visitor instantly realizes.

But I hold no grudge. In fact, if I may offer some constructive criticism, Mr. Morem, whenever I drive through your quaint town of log cabins and fishermen's shanties, I think, "You know, what Morro Bay needs, to really reach its potential, is a reroofing job."

As for the insulting nicknames? I phoned Morem, who told me that Central Coast towns tend to be laid-back about such matters.

"People can good-naturedly say 'Morro Bay — isn't that known as Moron Bay?' " Morem told me. And Los Osos is known as Los Grossos.

Yes, perhaps they're more advanced emotionally in Morro Bay than we are here in the Inland Valley.

On the other hand, there was a very interesting topic in the "letters to the editor" section next to Morem's column.

As it turns out, Morro Bay is about to embark on an exciting, cutting-edge experiment in traffic control.

They plan ... a roundabout. Just like Claremont put in and, after widespread confusion, derision and anger, sheepishly took out.

Oh, we'll have our revenge.

Who said Central Park couldn't be done? Oh yeah, the voters did

May 17, 2000

Hey, gang! Spent a week "getting away from it all" in Illinois — which is taking the idea to extremes, isn't it? — but I have to confess, I was anxious to get back. After all, while I was lolling around my parents' palatial estate in bustling Olney (population 10,000), voters in Rancho Cucamonga were surely shaking hands with Destiny.

It was hard to contain my excitement on May 9, knowing that 2,000 miles away, Cucamongans were bound to be approving Measure J, the tax that would make Central Park a reality.

"O, the glory we shall see, once the vision of the all-wise City Council is made manifest!" I thought each night, head upon my pillow, smiling dreamily as the veil of slumber descended. "A new Rome ... a modern-day Byzantium ... a beacon to the recreation-minded shall Cucamonga be ... zzzzzzzz..."

Now that I'm back, I guess it's only a matter of days

before the politicians line up in their hardhats and gold shovels to turn the first spade of dirt. Can 103 acres of fun be far behind?

Editor's note: Dave, you ninny, voters killed the park tax. It's deader than Elvis. Where have you been, the Midwest?

You're telling me Measure J lost?! Who could have predicted this?

Well, define "everybody."

Gee, and Central Park seemed like such a winner, too. I mean, who WOULDN'T want to pay $129 a year, forever, for an aquatic center, dog park, a tournament tennis court with grandstands and a pro shop — wow! — plus two lakes, pedestrian trails, picnic areas and open space?

Heck, Measure, J needed only 66.7 percent approval from voters. You'd figure 100 percent would back a great deal like this.

But you'd figure wrong. Two-thirds approval? They couldn't even get one-third.

In fact, an alarming 76 percent gave Central Park the ol' thumbs down.

The rabble isn't even that bloodthirsty in *Gladiator*.

Admittedly, the initial plans for the park might have been a tad, ah, excessive. You remember: a $166 million mega-park, costing $900 a year per person and boasting, among other amenities, waterfalls and a lecture hall and four — not one, not two, not three, but four — arts centers. Cucamonga, the Broadway of the West!

Now that even the $30 million version of the park has bitten the dust, no one's quite sure how to get Central Park built.

Maybe they'll try something more modest.

Don't like $129 a year?

How about $10 a year? We'll give you five soccer fields! But they'll be made of gravel.

Or maybe $1 a year! Yes, only one measly buck a year. Oh, lots of amenities.

We'll hack an "interpretive trail" through the underbrush. In the center of the park, you'll find: an outhouse.

In reality, while the community catches its breath, city officials are talking about interim uses like — this is true — grapevines or a water park. I've got an idea appropriate to the site.

A turkey farm.

A bane of newspaper staffs is the "progress edition" or iterations thereof. These are "special sections" to which everyone must contribute in spare moments while maintaining their regular output, and which exist primarily for the purpose of selling advertising, which of course pays our salaries, thus making the nature of the assignment even more irritating to the idealists among us.

In the spring of 2000, we published a highly unusual progress edition, "Visions of the 21st Century," with a series of news and feature stories about what the Inland Valley might be like in 2020. Did anyone out there save a copy?

I was asked to write a column, which in this case I did happily, because the assignment was so goofy. You'll find that piece next.

Illustrating it required photos of me in a space suit in a public place, namely, a Metrolink platform, dressed like some clod from the future. Oh, the humiliation. Like most embarrassing experiences in life, it made for a good column, which I wrote for my regular newspaper appearance. That's reprinted here as well, along with the photos for your snickering pleasure. (My regular column mug showed me with hand on chin, which is why I mimicked the pose in a space helmet.)

He boldly goes where no columnist has gone before – Work, 2020 style

photos by Tom Zasadzinski/Inland Valley Daily Bulletin

May 21, 2000

So they came to me asking for my thoughts on The Workplace of the Future — namely, what it might be like in 2020.

They came to the right visionary.

Because I see numerous differences in the workplace in 20 years — sweeping, structural, fundamental changes.

The top change I foresee in 2020 is that workplace vending-machine snacks will be even older than they are today.

In fact. in 2020 the No. 1 cause of workplace injury will be from chewing, and trying to digest, Fritos Corn Chips that were made during the Ford Administration.

Other than that, life may not change so drastically in the next 20 years. After all, the workplace is much the same today as it was in 1980, isn't it?

Well, OK, today we do have such wonders as fax machines, cellular telephones, e-mail, human resources departments and computer solitaire. We've done away with layoffs. Today, we have "rightsizing."

We have computers. Also, carpal tunnel syndrome.

Health insurance is no longer free — which is understandable, given that the cost to insure one employee is equal to the gross domestic product of Zaire.

And today's health care is provided by HMOs, or Health Mutilation Organizations.

So maybe I was wrong about the workplace not changing much since 1980. So sue me. (Please, don't!)

What might the workplace be like in 2020, then? Taking the idea seriously, I read the latest research papers on the subject. I consulted with leading experts. And I traveled the globe in search of "cutting edge" workplaces that might provide a glimpse into our future.

Unfortunately, I got drunk and left my notes in a bar in Istanbul, forcing me to make up the following story.

The workplace of 2020

It was a shaping up as a typical day for Adam-12.

As usual, his robot butler awakened him promptly at 6 a.m. After a quick shower-and-buffing, Adam-12 allowed his butler to dress him, gulped down his breakfast-burrito pill, kissed his sleeping wives goodbye and rushed out the door of his Ontario Millsville home, fishing his *Inland Valley Daily Bulletin* compu-disk out of the front yard wading pool with a sigh.

Yes, another typical day, Adam-12 thought, tapping his sparkly boot impatiently as he waited on the CommuTube platform.

Soon the bullet car whooshed to a stop inside the clear, Habitrail-like CommuTube. Passengers jammed their way inside and the car sped onward.

Traveling under smog-free skies, Adam-12 was rushed past the Inland Valley's gleaming spires into the heart of Los Angeles toward his job with Acme Amalgamations, for which he worked as a drone.

Moments later, his office monolith in sight, Adam-12 pushed the red button by his seat, which ejected him a soaring 60 feet into the air. From there he used his jet-pack to swoop to the office, lickety-split.

Greeting the secretary-bots with a friendly smile, Adam-12 was soon at his desk on the 2,253rd floor. He plugged himself in and checked his unconscious for z-mail. He found an "Urgent" message from his supervisor, which he quickly uploaded.

"Adam, got a great joke for you," the z-mail said with a chortle. "What's the difference between dating an undersea-dwelling atomic killer pervert cockroach and dating an attorney? At least with an undersea-dwelling atomic killer pervert cockroach, you can take it home to meet Mom! Har-har!"

After rolling his eyes, Adam-12 blinked twice for "delete." He sat back in his podchair and, donning his ether helmet, began amalgamating.

Ninety minutes later, Adam-12 took a break to visit the men's room. "What's new, Ed-9?" he asked a colleague.

"Same old, same old. Can you believe this weather?" Ed-9 said, shaking his head and chuckling. Turning to leave, he said: "Hey, have a good one."

Adam-12 rolled his eyes so hard, they momentarily got stuck. Looking in the mirror, he adjusted his pajamas. These "casual Mondays" are nice, but still too restrictive, he thought.

Over at Mega Incorporated, he thought bitterly, employees get "clothing optional Mondays."

Alter further amalgamating, it was lunch time! Adam-12

hooked up with Eve-3 and Henry-8 for a trip to Les Wok'd Taco, a fusion French-Asian-Mexican restaurant within easy jet-pack distance from the office.

Over his steaming escargot-and-eel-taco pill, Henry-8 complained about his wives. Eve-3 tuned him out, literally. Instead, she tuned in Adam-12 on the Thought Frequency.

>How about those Clippers?< Eve-3 asked.

>Can't believe they're in the playoffs a ninth straight year,< Adam-12 responded. >What a dynasty!<

>So get this, Adam ... Mary-16 told me 2,000 employees — the entire 3,511th floor — got "sent home early" this morning,< Eve-3 told him conspiratorially.

>Boy, I hate these buzz-words,< Adam-12 declared. >If people got rightsized, why won't the company just come out and say it? Let's call a shoveling implement a shoveling implement!<

"Adam," Henry-8 said, pointing to Adam-12's plate, "you're just picking at your sweet-and-sour-refried-crepes pill."

"Guess I'm not that hungry," Adam-12 said, putting down his straw. He buzzed for the waiter-bot and asked, "May I have a doggie bag?"

Back at the office, Adam-12 plugged himself in again and got down to business. That morning he had amalgamated 8,000 Acme accounts. Slacker, he thought. That young turk Jones-5 can do that in his sleep.

Oh, well, Adam-12 figured. I've been out of college only five months. Why stress? Another seven months and I'll be eligible for retirement anyway.

He linked with Acme's best client. "Hello, Wile E.!" Adam-12 said jovially. "How's life in the desert?"

"That roadrunner is driving me batty," the coyote told him. "Can you charge another anvil to my account?"

Mid-afternoon rolled around. Adam-12 checked his z-mail, then strolled to the company opium pipe to hear the latest gossip.

"Employees used to 'shoot the breeze' around something called a 'water cooler,'" said Alex-7, the company know-it-all, as he lay on the divan, puffing contentedly. "So have you heard anything new about the merger?"

Adam-12 lowered the Cone of Silence. "Just that Time-Warner-AOL-Viacom-Disney-Arco-Microsoft-Blimpie is still in negotiations to buy us," Adam-12 said.

"Eh?" Alex-7 said, cupping his hand behind his ear. "What's that?"

"Never mind," Adam-12 shouted, raising the Cone of

Silence in disgust. Adam-12 took the conveyor belt into the cafeteria. Mergers, z-mail, pill food ... life sure had changed since he was a lad back in 2000.

Absentmindedly, he dropped $5 into the vending machine for a bag of Fritos Corn Chips. He broke open the bag, grabbed a chip, put it in his mouth and bit down.

His scream of pain echoed throughout the 2,253rd floor.

Please, just photo shoot him now before the future arrives

photos by Tom Zasadzinski/Inland Valley Daily Bulletin

May 21, 2000

People often ask me if being a newspaper columnist is the easiest job on Earth. I respond by chuckling heartily, in the manner of William F. Buckley, or perhaps Beavis and Butt-head, while answering, "I WISH writing a column was so easy!"

Many factors lead to my answer. For one, my bosses might be reading this. But another is that my job sometimes requires me to do things that are a bit, ah, embarrassing.

Such as the other day, when a photo shoot called for me to walk the streets of Claremont while dressed — *sigh* — as a spaceman.

You see, for a special section titled "Visions of the 21st Century," I had penned a column on the workplace of the future. (The future, I boldly predict, will usher in all sorts of workplace innovations, among them, $5 vending-machine snacks.)

Someone had the brilliant idea of illustrating this column by dressing me in a futuristic, George Jetson-like costume and taking my picture and running it in the newspaper where everyone could see it and laugh, including my landlady, my dry cleaner and women I might someday wish to date.

I had no real problem with this concept. I'm a good sport. Besides, this shoot would take place in our newsroom photo studio. The sole witness would be a photographer. And surely, after a couple of days, they'd quit looking for his body.

So I agreed. And days later, I was in a costume shop in Rancho Cucamonga, slipping into a futuristic-looking white jumpsuit of the "one size fits all" variety.

Of course, "all" didn't include me. The cuffs fell a few inches above the ankle, thus hinting that even in the future, the prospect of flooding will remain a very real danger.

Despite all this, I wasn't especially concerned.

Then I found out the photographer had decided that a studio shoot wouldn't work nearly as well as one outdoors. Outdoors on a Metrolink train platform, in downtown Claremont, pretending like I was commuting to work in the future.

Yikes!

Sigh.

Oh, all right. I'm already in THIS deep, so why not?

(I felt like the frog who is boiled alive — not by being tossed into a pot of boiling water, but by having the temperature raised gradually so he doesn't realize what's happening to him.)

All too soon, the next morning arrived. I parked in the lot a block from the station.

Pulling the gold breastplate over my head, I locked my car, tucked my astronaut helmet under my arm and strode off in my white jumpsuit.

I passed by a parked police car and managed, somehow, to avoid arrest.

At the station, the photographer posed me near the tracks for a succession of shots under the curious eyes of a platform full of commuters. And a train full of passengers.

And assorted train conductors.

I would estimate the shoot took about 10 minutes, although they may have been the longest 10 minutes of my life.

So was the public embarrassment worth it? I would say yes, because as a columnist, sometimes it's necessary to suffer for my, ahem, art.

But you can judge for yourself. Advance reviews are promising.

"Nice column, Dave," one colleague chortled last week after seeing an early copy. "But that photo! Dude, you look like a SERIOUS dork."

Comments like those make it all worthwhile.

Wrestler Rowdy Roddy Piper turns out to be a hard man to pin down

May 24, 2000

So you may have heard that Rowdy Roddy Piper was supposed to come to the Grove Theatre this weekend. Now, I'm wrestling with how to break the bad news.

He's bowed out.

(Yes, Rowdy Roddy Piper the wrestling champion. Which Rowdy Roddy did you think I meant, the neuro-surgeon?)

Piper was scheduled to appear, one night only, on Saturday to benefit the Upland theater, which is owned by relatives of the late comedian Sam Kinison.

Usually the Grove features light, popular musicals. For instance, *A Chorus Line* opens June 3.

In the meantime, though, they booked — why not? — a professional wrestler.

I'm not sure what Rowdy Roddy was planning to do

in his one-man show. The Grove wasn't sure either. Who knows, maybe he'd play Clarence Darrow.

I was hoping to ask the Rowdy One himself. His personal assistant tentatively set up a phone interview for Monday afternoon. When I called, he said Roddy was rehearsing for the show right at the moment but would call me back shortly.

You have no idea how exciting this was.

"I'm going to interview Rowdy Roddy Piper!" I told the nearest colleague, all a-quiver.

He swiveled quickly in his chair.

"Who?" he asked blankly.

Undaunted, I did some research on Piper from various Internet sites. He was born Roderick Toombs in Scotland. He started wrestling at age 15 and he's still going at it at age 46.

He's probably best known for his 1985 grudge match with Hulk Hogan, dubbed "The War to Settle the Score" and which aired on MTV. (Pouts a pro-Piper Web site: "Hogan wins with help from Cyndi Lauper and Mr. T.")

Piper has also appeared in numerous movies, including something called *Hell Comes to Frogtown*. It probably doesn't live up to its title. How could it?

Armed with this information, I came up with interview questions. But Piper never called.

Hours later, I tried again and heard that the show may be postponed until after the Memorial Day holiday. They'd call by noon Tuesday, guaranteed, to let me know.

Around 2:30 Tuesday, having heard nothing, I put in another call. "It's up in the air," I was told.

Much like Piper when he's being twirled overhead by (snicker) Cyndi Lauper?

Two hours later, just as I was wrapping up this column, Rowdy Roddy called me. (Seriously!)

His bosses at World Championship Wrestling told him he doesn't have their approval to attend on Saturday, he said. He professed deep disappointment.

"God bless George Jones, but I'm not him. I don't miss engagements," Piper said. "I do intend to come on another date."

By the way, his one-man show will be titled "An Evening With Roddy Piper" and he hopes to take it on the road. In it, he'll talk about the colorful characters he's known over his 31 years in the, ah, sport.

Piper promises that when the Upland show is rescheduled, I'll be No. 1 on his list.

I'm not sure I like the sound of that.

Knight, Rocker Temper Tantrums Produce Hope for Anger-Impaired

June 7, 2000

So, have you heard the news on the Uncontrollable Anger front? First, basketball coach Bobby Knight was put on notice that he'll lose his job unless he stops throttling his players.

And on Monday, baseball pitcher/loose cannon John Rocker was sent down to the minors after doing what he does best: pitching a fit.

Tsk, tsk. I hear about these terrible, terrible incidents and shake my head. They fill me with one overriding emotion.

Envy.

Because I wish I had a bad temper. In fact, I wish I had a legendary temper. I know it's un-P.C., but people should have to watch what they say around me. Wrath of Khan? Hey, worry about the Wrath of Dave.

Unfortunately, I'm more like mild-mannered reporter Clark Kent, only without the he-man alter ego.

I polled some friends on whether they'd ever seen me fly into a rage. "No," Chuck said. He added helpfully: "But I HAVE seen you get peeved."

Great. Who am I — Niles Crane?

Monica has never seen me angry either. She said: "I've only seen you annoyed."

Well, that's better than peeved. Annoyance is just a notch below true anger, right?

Feeling a bit better, I posed the question to my friend Holly.

"You got mad at me once," she said.

Yes!! This was music to my ears. Please, Holly, give me the details, if it's not too, y'know, painful to relive the memory.

"I was drawing a map to give you directions and I kept saying 'go east,' even though I was pointing west," she recalled. "You said, 'You don't even know the difference between east and west!' That was the only time I've ever seen you angry."

I only get angry about points on a compass?

Now Bobby Knight, there's a role model.

He once tossed a chair across the basketball court. He stuffed a fan in a garbage can. He flipped off people in the stands.

And this is when he's holding back.

Even better, he once threw a vase at a secretary. He choked a player during practice. One time he even choked a man in a restaurant!

(People choke in restaurants all the time, but that's usually on chicken bones, or when they get the bill, not because someone's hands are wrapped around their throat.)

Now Knight's on the chopping block? I don't know what the world's coming to.

Then there's John Rocker. On Sunday he ran into a Sports Illustrated reporter — the one who wrote the story that got Rocker into all that trouble a few months ago.

Rocker went ballistic. He got in the reporter's face. Literally: Rocker turned his cap around to gain another couple of inches. He yelled for two minutes straight.

"This isn't over between us," Rocker railed. "Do you know what I can do to you?"

If only I'd been there to take notes.

I can't handle my non-anger. Maybe some celebrity should make a self-help tape for people like me. Like: "Go Nuts the Al Pacino Way."

In the meantime, while Knight and Rocker take anger management classes, I guess I'm stuck with the third-rate version.

Peeve management.

Many flubs, but (whew!) no 'Flubber'

June 18, 2000

Well, the American Film Institute list of the 100 funniest American movies is out, and some like it not.

Sure, *Some Like It Hot*, the 1959 comedy featuring Jack Lemmon and Tony Curtis dressed up as women, and Marilyn Monroe only partly dressed, is a worthy No.1. But *Tootsie* at No. 2?

That makes America's two funniest-ever movies ones whose theme is men wearing women's clothes. Who judged this thing, Martin Lawrence?

Those two aren't the only, ah, kinks in this list, which, like anything so subjective as "best" and "funniest," offers plenty to argue about.

The rest of the Top Ten: *Dr. Strangelove, Annie Hall, Duck Soup, Blazing Saddles, MASH, It Happened One Night, The Graduate* and *Airplane.*

All decent movies. But I'd drop *MASH* and *Airplane* toward the bottom of the Top 100 like anvils.

Thankfully, *Porky's* missed out entirely. But close examination of the Top 100 reveals plenty of examples of the 1,800 judges collectively slipping on a banana peel.

I don't want to start a pie fight, but what are *Ghostbusters, The Jerk, Mrs. Doubtfire* and *Moonstruck* doing on this list?

I did a slow bum when I realized that WC. Fields (*It's a Gift*, No. 58), Laurel and Hardy (*Sons of the Desert*, No. 96) and Bob Hope (*Road to Morocco*, No. 78) each have just one movie in the Top 100. Gee, just like fellow comedic genius Warren Beatty (*Shampoo,* No. 47)!

And with *Singin' in the Rain* looking slick at No. 16, hoofer Gene Kelly is funnier than almost everyone, including the Little Tramp. (No, not Erin Brockovich.)

In fact, poor Chaplin, whose *Gold Rush* is No. 25, is only a couple of notches funnier than the Farrelly Brothers' *There's Something About Mary* (No. 27). Talk about your sticky situations.

A lot of classics were nowhere to be found. Where were Buster Keaton's *Our Hospitality* and *Seven Chances*? Cary Grant and Katharine Hepburn's *Holiday*? Frank Capra's *You Can't Take It With You*? Jimmy Stewart and Margaret Sullavan's *Shop Around the Corner*? Stewart as an unarmed sheriff cleaning up the town in *Destry Rides Again*?

And why is Buster Keaton's laugh riot *The General* way down at No. 18?!

I'm so mad, I feel like spraying seltzer down someone's pants.

Maybe animation didn't count, since no cartoons made the list. Too bad, because funny is funny, and *Lady and the Tramp* should've been on there. Not to mention Bugs Bunny.

A few personal favorites missed the list, too. Steve Martin's *Roxanne*. Woody Allen's *Play It Again, Sam* and *What's Up, Tiger Lily?* (in which he took a cheesy Japanese spy movie and overdubbed a whole new plot).

On the bright side, there's plenty to smile about. The classics did far better on this list than on the AFI's best American movies poll two years ago.

The Marx Brothers, Chaplin and Preston Sturges get four movies apiece; not enough, but in the ballpark. Keaton gets three. Woody Allen gets five — none from the past 20 years, Woody take note.

And lots of my favorites made the list, from Bill Murray's *Groundhog Day* to Harold Lloyd's *The Freshman* to Albert Brooks' *Lost in America* — a movie whose "nest egg" speech nearly put me on the theater floor. (Now THAT'S a sticky situation.)

Even after all this, I haven't told you the best part of the list.

Want to know the best part of the list?

No Jim Carrey.

Ask Gene Guy About Human Genome

June 28, 2000

Did you hear the thrilling news? The human genome has been mapped!

Boy oh boy. I'm still shaking my head in wonder.

Honestly, when you were a child, did you ever dream we'd see the human genome mapped in our lifetime?

Of course you didn't. Before Monday, you thought "the human genome" was a rock band. "Gene" was the neighbor who never gave back your rake. And so, to make this amazing scientific breakthrough comprehensible to the average person, who is, frankly, not that bright, allow me to present another of my helpful, public-spirited Q & A features, "Ask the Gene Guy."

Dear Gene Guy: What is the human genome?

Answer: It's been described as the detailed instruction manual for the inner machinery of every member of our species.

Dear Gene Guy: Wow. Why haven't we had this instruction manual all along?

Answer: One was supposed to be included with every birth, but they messed up at the factory.

Dear Gene Guy: What does this instruction manual consist of?

Answer: The genome is made up of a four-letter code — A, T, C and G — repeated in different combinations in a string 3 billion letters long.

As you can imagine, this makes for some pretty tough reading, especially at the beach. Chapter One of the genome begins: "It was a dark and stormy ATCG AGCT TGCA."

Dear Gene Guy: We're made up of 3 billion letters? How different is one person from the next?

Answer: Individual humans share 99.9 percent of their DNA, meaning that we are far more alike than we are different. We are separated from each other by a mere 300,000 letters. But geneticists caution that at least 500,000 letters separate us from Angelina Jolie.

Dear Gene Guy: Are there 3 billion genes, too?

Answer: No. Science isn't sure yet how many genes there are, but estimates range from 30,000 to 140,000 — slightly more than you'll find at any Gap outlet.

Dear Gene Guy: What good and bad might come from mapping the genome?

Answer: We may eventually be able to cure terrible diseases, most of which have a genetic cause.

On the downside, expectant parents might create "designer babies" who are ideal in face, form and mind. Imagine, a whole world full of perfect people! Frankly, I don't need the competition.

Dear Gene Guy: Still, it sounds like science is just getting started on the genome. Will they ever make sense of this mass of information?

Answer: It might take a century before we decipher and truly comprehend all 3 billion letters. Some scientists pray for a shortcut.

Dear Gene Guy: A shortcut for reading the human genome? What shortcut is that?

Answer: They're hoping for a movie version.

A friend at the *Los Angeles Times* who wrote humor told me the next column was brilliant and that colleagues with whom he'd shared it had a similar reaction. To paraphrase our 45th president, that's what people say. I don't know, you tell me.

As you can imagine, praise from within the *L.A. Times*, when you're writing in semi-obscurity in the distant suburbs, was a boost to my confidence and morale. It didn't result in employment, but it was a boost.

Thomas Jefferson, You've Got Mail

July 5, 2000

In signing a bill that gives electronic contracts the same legal status as those written on paper and signed in ink, President Clinton said: "If this had existed 224 years ago, the Founding Fathers wouldn't have had to come all the way to Philadelphia on July Fourth for the Declaration of Independence. They could have e-mailed their John Hancocks in."—news reports, June 30

* * *

E-mail from: Thomas Jefferson

To: Second Continental Congress

Subject: Independence from England

Guys, here's the Declaration (see attachment, Decl). Please read. Hit reply to sign it. So simple!

* * *

From: John Hancock

To: Thomas Jefferson

Tom: Luv yr Decl. Count me in! Pls center my name right underneath and print in 24-pt type. I want King George to be able to read it without his spectacles. :-)

* * *

From: Francis Lightfoot Lee

To: Thomas Jefferson

Enjoyed Decl. of Independis (sp?). Am forwarding some inspirational aphorisms and hilarious blonde jokes. You'll love these!

* * *

From: Samuel Adams

To: Thomas Jefferson

Tom, can't get to attachment. HELP!!!

* * *

From: Thomas Jefferson

To: Samuel Adams

Sam, chill out. Have an ale. ;-)

Am resending Decl as text file. If you still can't get to it, Franklin posted it at www.peoplegottobefree.org.

* * *

From: Elbridge Gerry

To: Thomas Jefferson

cc: Mailing list

I'm in. Btw, have you been alerted to the new virus going around? It will wipe out all files. It arrives under the innocent name I Fancy You. Please, Tom, for the sake of our fledgling republic, back up your files.

* * *

From: William Williams

To: Thomas Jefferson

Pls double-check printing of my sig. The double name confuses the spell-check. It always wants to replace Williams (note the s) with William, so I end up William William. :-(

* * *

From: Button Gwinnett

To: Thomas Jefferson

cc: Second Continental Congress

Heard John Hancock sent in his "John Hancock." Fine. Now I'm sending in my "Button Gwinnett." Feel free to use this expression ("I'll just put my Button Gwinnett right here") in yr own transmissions, conversations, memoirs, blah blah blah. Perhaps it will yet catch on. Yrs hopefully, Button

* * *

From: John Adams

To: Thomas Jefferson

Nice job, Tom. Well, gotta run. I'm trying to catch the last matinee of *The Patriot*.

* * *

From: Benjamin Franklin

To: Thomas Jefferson

Did you get my last e-mail? My ISP, Colonies Online, keeps kicking me off. Before that my sig kept getting bounced back with USER ERROR. Don't output the Declaration w/o me!!!!!

 က ◈ က

Bee Guy bugs more than just insects

July 19, 2000

Well, I had to kill my housemates. Shocked? Don't be. It was either them or me, officer. Some of them I killed myself. I hired somebody to kill the rest. And I'm glad, do you hear? Glad!

POLICE: We'll take that as a confession, creep-o. Come along quietly.

No, wait! Stop! They were just flying insects!

I judged them to be hornets. A couple hundred of them moved in last month. They settled in the ceiling of my laundry room.

I didn't see them move in. I imagine they used professionals, or at least semi-professionals. All their loathsome little furnishings probably arrived in a little van. The logo on the side: Starving Larvae.

The first bug I saw was perched on a window in my laundry room, crawling around innocently. Because I am a soft-hearted humanitarian as well as an insectitarian, I opened the door and shooed it outdoors. Fly free, gentle creature, and go with God!

An hour later, I saw a second bug and, puzzled, shooed it

out. Later, a third.

The fourth I splattered with a rolled-up newspaper. I'm surprised the force of my blow didn't shatter the window.

For the next month, perhaps three insects a day would fly out of a crack in the ceiling and buzz around. Most fell victim to my newspaper, which I kept close at hand. Bug spray knocked out a bunch more.

A few saved me the trouble of killing them by flying directly into a light fixture, where they fried to death on the bulb. The light was definitely brighter than they were.

Finally, last week, the Bee Guy rode to my rescue. My landlady had called him. He knocked, I opened the door, and he said, by way of introduction, "You're not a woman. If you are, you're the ugliest woman I've ever seen."

I think the Bee Guy may have spent too much time around annoying insects. Their personality is rubbing off.

Anyway, the Bee Guy, who wore the traditional Bee Guy Garb of jumpsuit, hat and full-face netting, sized up the situation. They're not hornets, he announced, they're yellow jackets.

Yellow jackets? How chic. What is it, a nest of car salesmen?

After weighing their options, the Bee Guy and his aide, the Assistant Bee Guy, decided to get at the yellow jackets from the outside.

My landlady and I stayed inside, watching through the window as the Assistant Bee Guy used a crowbar to rip boards from the side of the house. At times like these, I am perfectly happy to be a renter, not a homeowner.

My landlady, trying to make conversation, politely asked

the Bee Guy how he got into the Bee Guy Business.

"God," he replied matter-of-factly.

Soon, the Assistant Bee Guy triumphantly pulled a comb, covered in yellow jackets, out of the wall and put it in a bag. Then he sprayed some goop onto the straggling yellow jackets, which began dropping from the laundry room ceiling like, uh, flies.

As they staggered around, I whacked them with the rolled-up newspaper. The Bee Guy re-entered the room. He casually squashed two yellow jackets with his bare index finger.

I quietly put the newspaper down.

After the Bee Guy got his money, I caught up with him in the driveway. Yellow jackets swooped around us, angry and homeless, as he climbed into his truck.

I asked him anxiously if there was anything I should know.

"There are a lot of things you should know," the Bee Guy said philosophically. "Can you be more specific?"

So, officer, my dead housemates are just yellow jackets. No concern of yours.

But the Bee Guy is lucky he didn't hang around another five minutes.

A STIFF UPPER LIP LOOSENS

August 13, 2000

Britain's Queen Mother turned 100 on Aug. 4, smiling and waving and remaining characteristically silent. She has not given an interview in 77 years. — news accounts

DAVID ALLEN: Greetings, Your Highness. Thank you for granting me your first interview since 1923.

QUEEN MOTHER: Hhhrrraaaggghhh.

D.A.: Pardon?

Q.M.: Cough, cough. My apologies. I haven't even spoken since 1982.

D.A.: My first question is, why are you breaking your 77-year silence?

Q.M.: I have a lot to get off my chest.

D.A.: Such as?

Q.M.: The Labour Party. Those socialists led our country to ruin. James Ramsay MacDonald should be hanged for founding that party.

D.A.: That was 1924.

Q.M.: Yes, and it's been eating away at me ever since.

D.A.: What else?

Q.M.: Wallis Simpson. Edward threw away the monarchy for that wretched woman. She was morally loose. Once I saw her in a bathing suit that exposed her knees!

D.A.: Shameful. Care to remark upon British culture?

Q.M.: Yes. I'm still mad at Yoko.

D.A.: You liked the Beatles?

Q.M.: Oh, dear, yes. Four quite charming lads. Although I felt that later works such as *The White Album*, while superficially more mature, were ironically less inventive than the early, disarmingly simple hits.

D.A.: You are full of surprises, Queen Mum. Now, what of the royal family? Surely their shenanigans have caused you a lot of grief.

Q.M.: See, misconceptions like those are why I decided to speak out. The royals are delightful, all of them. Although I found Diana a bit homely. Especially compared to my lovely grandson, Charles.

D.A.: Uh, certainly. Anything else bugging you?

Q.M.: The Americans! They've made us look positively evil in that Revolutionary War motion picture, *The Patriot*. Yet they have no qualms about stealing our best TV show, *Who Wants to be a Millionaire*. Mark my words, if those upstart Americans don't mind their manners, I may order their country recolonized.

D.A.: Forgive me, but as an American, I take umbrage at these intemperate remarks.

Q.M.: American? I was told you were from the *London Times*, the paper I hand-picked as my forum for breaking my 77-year silence.

D.A.: Oh. There must have some mix-up.

Q.M.: Mix-up?

D.A.: I'm a humor columnist from California.

Q.M.: GUARDS! OFF WITH HIS HEAD!

ꕥ ◈ ꕥ

The 2000 Democratic Convention took place in Los Angeles, at Staples Center, and the *Daily Bulletin*, flexing its muscles, provided some coverage. I got to attend two days and write columns, a small thrill. And to get there I rode Metrolink, which I was just beginning to master.

My model for this assignment was Dave Barry, the syndicated weekly humor columnist, who filed daily columns from the Winter Olympics with a combination of observation, interviews and exaggeration that still captured the truth of the experience. Could I do something similar?

The first column, based on observation and an interview, was written at my desk the day after the experience. The second, which was almost entirely fanciful, was written on deadline on a desktop computer in the Staples press area. The minder and I couldn't get the email function to work, so I had to dictate the finished column by phone to an editor in Ontario, like it was the 1940s.

Both columns turned out okay, and I felt like I passed a test, if only in my own mind, that my style was flexible enough to handle a national news event in a humorous way.

Earnest meets Officer Friendly

August 15, 2000

Los Angeles — Monday was Day One of the Democratic National Convention and I can report from firsthand experience that by midday, despite the presence of thousands of protesters, the city was NOT in flames.

Of course, later in the evening an outdoor concert was scheduled by a provocative band called Rage Against the Machine, performing songs from their album *The Battle of Los Angeles*, so if the city burst into flames after my deadline, forget I said anything.

Based on fears of another unruly Seattle protest, everyone was expecting disaster from the get-go. (If not from the protesters, then from the *Daily Bulletin*, sending me to help cover the convention.)

Certainly the LAPD — motto: "To protect, serve and frame" — had predicted doom. They originally planned to force the protesters to stay a full block from Staples Center. From Staples, protesters would have looked not like people waving placards but like ants waving Post-It notes.

Luckily for the First Amendment, the judge who was asked to rule on the LAPD's plan rejected it immediately. Well, as soon as he stopped laughing.

So protesters now can occupy a parking lot directly across from Staples. However, there is a metal fence separating them from convention-goers. And you can only get in or out of the protest zone from one intersection. They're still isolated.

On the plus side, they have a sound system so powerful it can drop pigeons from the sky.

The protest zone is a colorful scene, when people are actually there. It seems to work like this: Protesters mobilize at Pershing Square, march to the protest zone and focus on one issue for an hour. Then they march back to Pershing Square, marshal forces for the next issue and return to the protest zone.

At 11 a.m., the asphalt was nearly devoid of life. A man at the podium on the concert-style stage was talking about immigration. He had an audience of a dozen.

Fifteen minutes later, a horde of people arrived on foot. Let the political theater begin!

"Theater" in a literal sense, because several protesters marched in with puppets. Not hand puppets, like Kukla, Fran and Ollie. These were towering, papier-mache puppets, worn like costumes.

One puppet was a menacing, black-clad police officer, perhaps 10 feet tall. The arms were operated by two people walking alongside. One arm waved a club. The other waved a flamethrower.

When the suit came off, out emerged a perspiring Laurel Dykstra of Seattle. What was it like in there, Laurel?

"It was very warm," Laurel admitted, "but it's worth it to draw attention to the criminalization of poor people and the militarization of the police."

One thing you have to say about protesters: They're the most earnest people you'll ever meet.

Puppets are reviving the art of the street protest. Laurel said hers is named Officer Friendly. She brought it on the bus from Seattle and plans to also use it at protests over the death penalty and the Rampart scandal. That is one busy puppet.

The protest at that moment? It was explained, sort of, by placards that read: "Gore: Oxy Out of U'wa Land!"

Their shorthand sounds like a particularly baffling newspaper headline, such as "Feds Eye Rail Pact." What the slogan meant is that Gore, a major Occidental Petroleum stockholder, should tell Occidental to forget about drilling for oil in land in Colombia settled by the U'wa tribe.

I confess I had never heard of the U'was, who were described from the podium as "5,000 traditional, voluntarily isolated indigenous people." (I suppose that means they don't get cable.)

From the podium, an organizer asked everyone to march in an orderly manner back to the staging area. "We're going to Pershing Square!" he said. "Follow the puppets!"

And so several hundred untraditional, involuntarily isolated, non-indigenous people marched up Figueroa Street.

OK, so I've poked fun. But I suspect that inside Staples Center, convention-goers were also following puppets, only they weren't wise enough to know it.

Cerebration Time; C'mon, Strike Up the Bland

August 18, 2000

Los Angeles — On Thursday, Albert "W." Gore accepted his party's nomination as president in a burst of characteristically thrilling rhetoric, offering a sweeping vision of America as "overall, pretty nice."

In his speech before dozing delegates at the Democratic National Convention, Gore took strong stands on the contentious issues of diversity, education and safety, which he is for. But he also offered specific proposals that give a hint of the type of president he would be.

He pledged to put 100,000 new school buses on the streets "so that no child is left behind."

And, emphasizing his work to save the environment, Gore promised "prosperity with a porpoise."

The not-especially-anticipated speech, which clocked in at 63 minutes but which analysts said seemed to last days, was seen as Gore's best chance to step into the spotlight after eight years as secretary of commerce.

Gore's ties to President Clinton may prove more hindrance than help.

Clinton, who is trying to help him however he can, on Thursday offered Gore his biggest boost yet: He endorsed Gore's rival, George W. Bush.

In a hastily called news conference, Clinton wagged his finger and told reporters: "I did not have electoral relations with that man, Mr. Gore."

Among Democratic leaders, expectations for Gore's speech ran high.

Democratic National Committee Chairman Terry McAuliffe told reporters, "This will be Gore's chance to show America what he is made of." Asked for a best guess as to what Gore is made of, McAuliffe answered, "It appears to be knotty pine."

Gore's blandness is a double-edged sword. According to a recent Field Poll, Americans believe he is generally decent. But 59 percent said they feel he is "possibly a robot."

Throughout the four-day convention, supporters tried several strategies to humanize Gore.

A 20-minute documentary film titled *Al Gore: The Man Behind the Magic* was played on giant video screens in the convention hall Thursday, telling the inspirational story of Gore's rise to prominence from his humble origins as a box of spare parts.

Gore's longtime friends also joined the effort, offering revealing anecdotes about the nominee during their convention speeches.

College roommate Tommy Lee Jones said he and Gore spent many an hour discussing their philosophy of life while being totally baked on marijuana.

And the candidate's wife, "Tepid" Gore, said that after a

hard day doing whatever it is he does, her husband loves to unwind by playing wacky practical jokes. After he is completely unwound, he said, she puts a giant key in his back and winds him up again.

Meanwhile, in the protest zone across from Staples Center, tensions mounted Thursday as hundreds of protesters focused their attention on their latest cause: protesting the end of the protests.

"With the convention ending, we will have to return home," one protester said from the stage set up in the protest zone, to shouts of assent. "We call on the Democratic National Convention to continue so that we may continue protesting!"

Waving signs that read "Four More Years," which apparently referred to the length they would like the convention to last, protesters chanted in unison, "No convention, no life! No convention, no life!"

"America is the richest country in the world, yet throughout America and right here in the streets of Los Angeles, people are starving for attention," said protester Ann Kempt. "It's in fascist corporate America's best interests to shut down this convention so they can shut down these protests."

(Reached at home in suburban Virginia, fascist corporate America declined comment.)

As unrest grew among protesters, police amassed along Figueroa Street in a show of force. When protesters refused to disperse, police brought out their most dreaded weapon: They turned on the giant video monitor outside Staples, broadcasting Gore's acceptance speech at 80 decibels.

Protesters nearest the video monitor were felled instantly by the sound of Gore's droning voice. Others tried to flee, but most could not escape the speech's powerful narcotic effect. "Fiends!" one man yelled at police, spraying vinegar in a futile attempt to dispel the clouds of torpor.

Police defended their aggressive response. "We had to take decisive action to restore order," said LAPD Cmdr. Dave Kalish, who said officers had been equipped with earplugs to avoid falling victim to Gore's speech themselves.

Thus ended the 2000 Democratic National Convention, which again focused the world's attention on Los Angeles after years marked by riots, earthquakes and economic recession. Haven't we suffered enough?

THEIR FINAL ANSWER IS 'NO'

August 20, 2000

The Japanese version of ABC's "Who Wants to Be a Millionaire" has been a ratings bust — apparently because Japanese culture has traditionally discouraged individuals from flaunting wealth. — news reports

ANNOUNCER: And now, please welcome the host of *Who Has a Yen to Be Rich*, Regisan Philbinaki!

CROWD: *(claps politely)*

HOST: Thank you for that warm greeting. Let's bring out our contestant, who will be competing for a top prize of 1 million yen!

ANNOUNCER: Please welcome Hiroshi Otaka!

CROWD: *(claps politely)*

HOST: It says here, Hiroshi, that you support your wife, her parents and four children on your modest salary as a counterman at a fast-food restaurant, Teriyaki Bell. What would you do if you won 1 million yen?

CONTESTANT: I fear I would have to change my name out of embarrassment at my sudden riches, Regisan.

HOST: Ha ha! What a kidder! Here's the first question: For 25,000 yen, is a softball question one that is A) easy, B) hard, C) about sports, or D) pitched underhanded?

CONTESTANT: The answer is A) easy!

HOST: Final answer?

CONTESTANT: Yes, Regisan.

HOST: You've just won 25,000 yen!

CROWD: *(claps politely)*

HOST: Shall we go for 50,000 yen?

CONTESTANT: *(hesitates)* I suppose that would not hurt.

HOST: All right, Hiroshi. For 50,000 yen, which of these is not the color orange: A) orange, B) orange, C) lime-green, or D) orange?

CONTESTANT: Regisan, it is C.

HOST: You've just won 50,000 yen!

CROWD: *(claps politely)*

HOST: Hiroshi, how do you feel?

CONTESTANT: My good fortune is making me queasy.

HOST: Ha ha! Let's move on the next level ... 100,000 yen!

CONTESTANT: *(moans audibly)*

HOST: For 100,000 yen, what is a number between 5 and 7: A) 4, B) 8, C) 6, or D) Lithuania?

CONTESTANT: I would like to phone a friend, Regisan.

HOST: Which friend will you be phoning?

CONTESTANT: My father.

HOST: Do we have Mr. Otaka on the line?

FATHER: Hello, Regisan. How may I help my son?

CONTESTANT: Father, we have just 15 seconds. I have won 50,000 yen on this quiz show. If we get the right answer to this question, I will win 100,000 yen!

FATHER: What do you need with 100,000 yen? Your greed shames me, my son. I do not know you anymore.

CONTESTANT: Father!!

FATHER: Do not call me again, you wealth-flaunter. (*click*)

CONTESTANT: Father!!

HOST: Some folks can't handle it when people they know become outlandishly wealthy, eh, Hiroshi? Looks like you'll have to answer this question on your own.

CONTESTANT: *(in tears)* I am walking away, Regisan.

HOST: You want to walk away with the 50,000 yen you've won?

CONTESTANT: No, just the initial 25,000 yen is fine. I will put it in the bank and earn a conservative rate of return, nothing flashy. Now, if you'll excuse me, I must begin to make amends among my family and neighbors for even participating in this stupid show.

HOST: And that ends another exciting episode of *Who Has a Yen to Be Rich*! As usual, the answer seems to be: no one!

CROWD: *(claps politely)*

We're A-No. 1, Top of the Heap, the Valedictorian, King of the Hill – in Smog

September 6, 2000

Regrettably, our region's national reputation has taken a beating in recent years. But I'm proud to report that we're turning things around. Start spreadin' the news: L.A. is back, baby!

Because of the Democratic National Convention, you ask? A booming economy? Rising home values?

Sorry, but no. If you want to know why things are looking up, just look up.

I'm referring to our air. It's the worst in the country again, which makes us the best in the country again.

Even the usually gloomy *Los Angeles Times* greeted the news with the celebratory headline "LA Tops Houston as Nation's Smoggiest City."

Yep, we're No. 1! Who says newspapers never print good news?

As you may recall, a year ago, in a shameful turn of events, we dropped to No. 2. Yep, in 1999, Houston stole our crown, posting 52 days of unhealthful ozone, compared with a puny 41 in LA.

This is what overconfidence can do. Assuming we would always have the country's worst air, we rested on our laurels. Predictably, we lost our title to an upstart. We became runner-up to, of all places, Houston — which sources tell me is a city in Texas. How embarrassing.

(Maybe this explains why Gov. George W. Bush is always making weird pronouncements like "We have to make the pie higher" — the Texas ozone is making him loopy.)

But this is no time for mirth, not when everything L.A. has ever stood for is going into the dumper.

We haven't had a good earthquake in years. Our riots have been reduced to "melees." I can't remember the last time Malibu burned.

And now, thanks to our misguided efforts to clean up our air, we might lose another of our signature elements — our robust, hearty, earth-toned air.

What are we going to do next, pave the beaches?

Luckily, the city of second chances is living up to its motto. Because, in yet another amazing only-in-L.A. turnaround, our smog this year has put us back on the charts and ahead of Houston.

As of late last month, our air exceeded limits for ozone 34 days, compared to a measly 26 for Houston. Hah! Eat our particulate matter, Houstonites.

This is the comeback of the year. But it's not over 'til it's over. We can still have a September swoon, chalk up only a couple of ozone-rich days and lose the smog title to a hard-charging, hard-breathing Houston.

But if we keep our eyes on the prize, give 110 percent and emulate the Lakers, we'll bring home a second national championship title this year. Go, L.A.!

At this point, you're probably saying, "David, we want this bad-air title so badly we can taste it. (The title AND the air.) What can we ordinary-schmoe Inland Valley citizens do to help?"

Good question! Because we solo commuters can't do it alone. It's going to take a lot of unnecessary vehicle trips, a lot of smoky barbecues and a lot of sitting at stoplights with our engines idling before we can claim victory.

A few quick tips (please post in a visible place):

If the nightly temperature drops below 65 degrees, start a roaring fire in the fireplace. That SUV you've had your eye on? Buy it, and quickly. And next time you plan to stock up on groceries in one big shopping trip, please, consider making numerous small purchases instead.

Why are your individual efforts important? Because there are quitters out there who take one look toward the mountains, realize they can't even see the mountains because of the curtain of smog, and decide they've done more than enough already.

Frankly, it's that attitude that cost us the title last year.

Friends, it's time to rally 'round the smog. If we put aside our petty differences, if we pull together for the greater good, if we emit enough deadly hydrocarbons, we can soon be back on top.

No. 1 again! It's enough to bring tears to your eyes. Coincidentally, so is our smog.

At least one reader wasn't amused by the following column on the topic of which was hotter in September 2000, the Inland Valley or hell. And he was a (gulp) minister.

"I was rather shocked how flippant you were about such a serious subject," the Calvary Chapel associate pastor scolded me by letter. "David, hell or Hades is nothing to joke about."

Criticism was the price I paid for being on the cutting edge of comedy. Later, as second, third and subsequent jokes were made about hell being hot, the average person no doubt came to take such humor in stride. But where was I by then? Forgotten, like all the other innovators.

Precisely How Hot Is It in Hades?

September 20, 2000

Look, I know it's hot. We all know it. What bugs me is how people keep mopping their brow and saying "It's hotter than hell." Like they would know!

Have any of them ever bothered to compare temperatures in the Inland Valley and hell before making this oh-so-casual observation? "Gosh darn the gol-durn blankety-heck!" I exclaimed, frightening my newsroom colleagues, who are delicate souls unused to such coarse language. "Nothing makes me madder than people who won't do their research."

And so I decided to investigate the situation first-hand.

I visited hell.

Climbing into a handbasket — the fastest way to get there, I'm told — I was transported through Time and Space until landing with a thud in what appeared to be an underground cave.

Lit by torches embedded in the stone walls, hell was a cavernous place that seemed to stretch on into infinity.

I tapped the first demon I met on the shoulder. "You know," I said, trying to make conversation, "I love this high ceiling."

He leaned on his pitchfork and spat. "Sure, it looks nice. But it's hell to heat in the winter. Literally."

I nodded sympathetically and moved on. Following the sound of lost souls doomed to eternal torment, I stepped into the cavern's nearest chamber. A naked man was chained to a rock while birds plucked at his intestines. He motioned me over.

"Water..." he gasped.

"No thanks," I replied, patting his shoulder, "I'm not thirsty."

But all this chitchat wasn't getting me anywhere. Whipping out my notepad, I strode into the next chamber, where a woman was being roasted over hot coals.

"Excuse me, miss," I said, "but how would you describe the heat?"

She responded with a bloodcurdling scream.

I looked up, pen poised over my notepad.

"How many h's in 'Yaaaahhhh!!!'?" I inquired.

Just then, a demon entered and suggested that if I wanted some hard facts on the temperature, I ought to talk to his supervisor. Eager to make some headway, I agreed.

The demon led me past the Lake of Fire, where people were bobbing up and down in boiling lava, shrieking in pain. I waved hello to some of my former editors. Gee, but it was nice to see them again!

"It must get hot down here," I remarked to one bather, who was being forced to towel off with a sheet of sandpaper.

He shrugged and said, "It's a dry heat."

Soon the demon and I were standing before a door marked "Private — Supervisor." Ushered inside, I encountered a red-faced man — well, he looked red all over, actually — in suspenders behind a desk, mopping his brow with a hanky.

An electric fan was set on high. On the wall was a travel poster of Canada's snow-capped peaks.

"Brrr!" I said involuntarily, stepping out of the fan's chilly path and smoothing my tie.

"You've barely broken a sweat!" the supervisor exclaimed, stamping his cloven hoof once in amazement. "How do you do it?"

"Well, I live and work in the Inland Valley," I explained apologetically. "I don't have air conditioning at home or in my car. And I've spent the past few days baking under the sun at the L.A. County Fair in Pomona."

He looked impressed and handed me a job application.

The Inland Valley, he said, is the perfect training ground for employment in Hades.

"Alter all," he admitted, "it's hotter than hell up there."

Wrestling Job Is a Real Croc

September 24, 2000

Not to burden you with my problems, but it's not easy being an incisive, hard-hitting humor columnist. You have no idea of the pressure I'm under! That's why I'm thinking about getting out of this game while the getting's good. Maybe it's time to retire and try something new.

But what would I do? All I've ever done is write for newspapers. Well, I delivered pizzas in high school, but not all that successfully. Often I would forget to bring one item, like the liter of soda, but the customer would insist, so I would have to make a second trip. How embarrassing.

Well, let's check the classifieds. Hmm ... here are two intriguing possibilities, and as luck would have it, both say no experience is required! The jobs:

1. Alligator wrestler.

2. International movie star.

I'm not kidding. The Seminole Indians in Florida are looking for an alligator wrestler, European filmmaker Roman Polanski is looking for a leading man, and they've both made the news because they're advertising in the newspaper classifieds.

The Seminoles put this "help wanted" ad in the *Fort Lauderdale Sun-Sentinel*: "WANTED: Alligator wrestlers. Must be brave and a risk taker. Males and females OK. No experience needed."

Why do they say "No experience needed"? What, have all the experienced alligator wrestlers already been eaten?

No experience is needed to star in Polanski's next movie, either. He's seeking a 25- to 35-year-old male through a classified in Britain's *Guardian* newspaper that advises potential leading men thusly: "Acting experience not essential but he needs to be sensitive, vulnerable and charismatic."

Is he looking for an actor or a date?

Just kidding, Roman. I loved *Rosemary's Baby* and *Chinatown* and all your movies in the 25 years since then (the titles escape me).

Let's schedule the audition. I'll be so sensitive, vulnerable and charismatic, you'll be crying buckets. But I guess we'll have to do this overseas, given that you're still, ahem, a wanted man in this country.

Now, I understand your movie's working title is *The Pianist*. Are you open to some tinkering? Because *The Pianist* — well, it's subtle, it's arty, it's Roman Polanski, but frankly, it won't play in Ontario. I'm thinking more along the lines of *Booty Shake*.

Oh, and Roman, about the plot. From what I've read, your movie is based on the autobiography of Polish composer Wladyslaw Szpilman. He escaped death in a Nazi concentration camp. Sounds like an intense, inspiring drama illustrating the triumph of the human spirit.

One question: Does he get the girl?

Boy, at this point I could use some career counseling. What a dilemma — international movie star or alligator wrestler? Maybe I should hedge my bets and apply for both.

About alligator wrestling. The way I understand it, the Seminole Nation does it to entertain vacationing rubes. Only no Seminoles want to wrestle alligators anymore. Seems all the young Seminoles are trying to get real jobs.

That's the problem with our young people today — no sense of tradition.

So the Seminole Nation is seeking outsiders. They're holding tryouts. (If they reject you, do they extinguish your torch and say, "The tribe has spoken"?)

You get a salary, you get benefits. Everything sounds good so far. I have just one lingering worry: The Seminoles never say what happened to the last alligator wrestler.

END OF A TRIVIAL PURSUIT

December 24, 2000

L.M. Boyd is retiring "Footnotes," his nationally syndicated column of useless facts and clipped writing, as of Dec. 30, leaving the Daily Bulletin *without one of its most popular features.*

Herewith, a tribute.

Q. My grandma used to joke that tiny objects were "smaller than a hummingbird's tonsils." How small are hummingbird tonsils, anyway?

A. Awfully small. Experts say 1/64th of an inch. Would hate to do the tonsillectomy.

* * *

Al Gore's precise margin of victory: 539,897 votes. Same as the number of redheads in New Jersey.

* * *

Goats are a vegetable.

* * *

Our History man says the 13th century is considered bad luck, so many history books go directly from the 12th to the 14th centuries.

* * *

Q. Alabama is our No. 1 maker of beef jerky. Who's No. 2?

A. Tennessee, No. 2. No. 3, my Uncle Buck.

* * *

Am often asked if any link between Rolodex and Rolo candy. Is one: Both used by actress Esther Rolle.

* * *

Cozy saying tells us "home is where the heart is." Goes back to Edgar Allan Poe. Heart, he wrote, was in the home, buried under floorboard, still beating.

* * *

Aluminum is a fruit.

* * *

Q. Everyone knows the phrase "by the skin of one's teeth," meaning a narrow escape from danger. Origin, please?

A. In olden times, teeth were covered with skin.

* * *

Tomatoes have their own form of government.

* * *

In an untamed portion of Kenya, the locals worship a goddess described as beneficent, glowing and perky. Her Kenyan name is unpronounceable. You'd know her as Britney Spears.

* * *

What's love got to do with it? A lot. Up to 92 percent, science tells us.

* * *

No, the Earth isn't round.

* * *

Niña, Pinta and Santa Maria, as all schoolchildren know, are Columbus' three ships. Historians rarely mention Columbus' fourth boat, Monkey Business.

* * *

"Unsightly hair": a redundancy.

* * *

That pink crescent under your fingernails? Surprise, surprise — it's actually the tip of a whole other fingernail that starts back at your knuckle. Or so claims the guy next to me at the bar.

* * *

Q. Oil and water don't mix. Why not?

A. Too shy.

* * *

"Jack Sprat would eat no fat, his wife would eat no lean" goes the nursery rhyme. Rhyme doesn't record family cholesterol levels.

* * *

Sharks deadly man-eaters? Quite the opposite. Many live off flowers.

* * *

Q. Mr. Boyd, what will you do in retirement?

A. Clean up on *Millionaire*!

That brings us to the end of *Getting Started*, the best of my first four years of columns. To anticipate your possible reaction: Yes, this really was the best I could do. Thanks for asking!

If the preceding pages haven't turned you off my work completely, look for my other book, *Pomona A to Z*, and for my current writing in the *Inland Valley Daily Bulletin* (in print of course, and online at www.dailybulletin.com). Those columns and more can also be found on my blog (www.insidesocal.com/davidallen) and on my Facebook page (www.facebook.com/davidallencolumnist). More books are expected, and publication of this one provides the motivation. Namely, this early crud can't be what I go out on!

Acknowledgments

Under the theory that real books have Acknowledgments pages, this one will have one too. In the spirit of full disclosure, we didn't do one for *Pomona A to Z*, which I hope didn't affect your enjoyment, or for that matter sales.

First, let me acknowledge the editors, reporters and photographers with whom I worked in this period, some of whom became friends as well as work colleagues, and some of whom displayed a dedication, kindness and quick wit that were an inspiration. Others, not so much.

Special thanks to Laura Lemmon, who hired me at the *Bulletin* at the encouragement of her husband, Russ, with whom I worked in Victorville; Rob Wagner, who ran a lively, edgy newsroom; Frank Pine, who gave me a regular weekly slot and also approved the use of columns for this book; Mike Brossart, who gave me a second weekly slot; and Christia Gibbons, who as city editor offered consistent support and encouragement in this period. I asked her to write the foreword since we're still in touch, and it turns out she's still ready with support and encouragement.

For this book, my thanks to photographer John Valenzuela for his creativity and good humor on a hot summer afternoon for the photo shoot that resulted in this cover, to publisher Mark Givens, for his design, patience and interest, and to various Starbucks locations and the Pomona coffeehouse Mi Cafecito for sustenance, writing space and wifi. Is it too late to give Sally Egan a shout-out for her cover photo for *Pomona A to Z*, and to her dad, Larry Egan, for hosting the launch party for that book, not to mention commissioning a banner for the occasion? Let's hope not.

Lastly, let me acknowledge the late Steve Julian for his foreword to *Pomona A to Z*. Steve, KPCC-FM's morning anchor and a native of Pomona, died in 2016. Having him as part of my first book assumed larger significance once he was no longer with us. I don't have much to remember him by, mostly the memory of a few leisurely, collegial lunches in and around Pomona, but I have his foreword as part of my book forever, and that gives me a glow.

About David Allen

David Allen, a native of Illinois, has worked in newspapers for three decades, all in California, his adopted home. His career began in 1987 at the *Santa Rosa News Herald* and continued at the *Rohnert Park-Cotati Clarion*, *Petaluma Argus-Courier* and *Victor Valley Daily Press*, some of which are still in business. In 1997 he joined the *Inland Valley Daily Bulletin*, where he is a columnist. Find his work online at dailybulletin.com, or impress your friends by buying an actual newspaper. A resident of Claremont, he is the author of one previous book, *Pomona A to Z*, also from Pelekinesis.

www.ingramcontent.com/pod-product-compliance
Lightning Source LLC
Chambersburg PA
CBHW020324170426
43200CB00006B/268

* 9 7 8 1 9 3 8 3 4 9 4 9 2 *